MICROBIOLOGY BSC NURSING 1ST YEAR

PREVIOUS YEAR NURSING CHAPTER WISE SOLVED QUESTION PAPERS

RUTWIK UPENDRA BHALSHANKAR

ISBN 979-888606430-8

Contents

CHAPTER ONE

INTRODUCTION

Q 1. Define the term microbiology.

= Microbiology is the study of living organisms of microscopic size.

Or

Microbiology is the branch of science that is concerned primarily with the **biology** of microorganisms and their effects on other living organisms.

"Father of Microbiology". Contributions of Louis Pasteur in Microbiology are very important.

Q 2.Contributions of Louis Pasteur in Microbiology.

= Father of microbiology—Louis Pasteur is

known as "Father of microbiology" because his contribution led to the development of microbiology as a separate scientific discipline.

Contributions of Louis Pasteur in Microbiology :

1. Coined the term Microbiology ; Pasteur coined

the term microbiology for the study of living organisms of microscopic size.

2. Proposed germ theory of disease ; He established that putrefaction and fermentation was the result of microbial activity and that different types of fermentations were associated with different types of microorganisms .

3. Disapproved theory of spontaneous generation ;

He disapproved the theory of spontaneous generation in . In a series of classic experiments, Pasteur proved conclusively that all forms of life, even microbes, arose only from their like and not de novo.

4. Developed sterilization techniques ;

He introduced sterilization techniques and developed the steam sterilizer, hot-air oven and autoclave in the course of these studies.

5. Developed methods and techniques for cultivation of microorganisms

6. Studies on pebrine (silkworm disease), anthrax, chicken cholera and hydrophobia.

7. Pasteurization ;

He devised the process of destroying bacteria, known as pasteurization (1863-65). This process (pasteurization) is employed to preserve milk and certain other perishable foods throughout the civilized world today.

8. Coined the term vaccine ;

It was Pasteur who coined the term vaccine for such prophylactic preparations to commemorate the first of such preparations namely cowpox, employed by Jenner for protection against smallpox.

9. Discovery of the process of attenuation and chicken

cholera vaccine ; An accidental observation that chicken cholera bacillus cultures left on the bench for several weeks lost their pathogenic, property but retained their ability to protect the birds against subsequent infection by them, led to the discovery of the process of attenuation and the development of live vaccines.

10. Developed live attenuated anthrax vaccine .

11. Developed rabies vaccine.

12. Noticed Pneumococci—Pneumococci were first noticed by Pasteur and Sternberg independently in 1881.

Q 3. Koch postulates / principles of microbiology.

= Koch's postulates

Koch's postulates are a series of guidelines for the experimental study of infectious disease. According to these, a microorganism can be accepted as the causative agent of an infectious disease only if the following conditions are satisfied:

Postulate 1: The organism should be regularly found in the lesions of the disease.

Postulate 2: It should be possible to isolate the organism in pure culture from the lesions.

Postulate 3-Inoculation of the pure culture into suitable laboratory animals should reproduce the lesion of the disease.

Postulate 4 : It should be possible to reisolate the organism in pure culture from the lesions produced in the experimental animals.

Subsequently an additional fifth criterion introduced states that specific antibodies to the organism should be demonstrable in the serum of patients suffering from the disease .

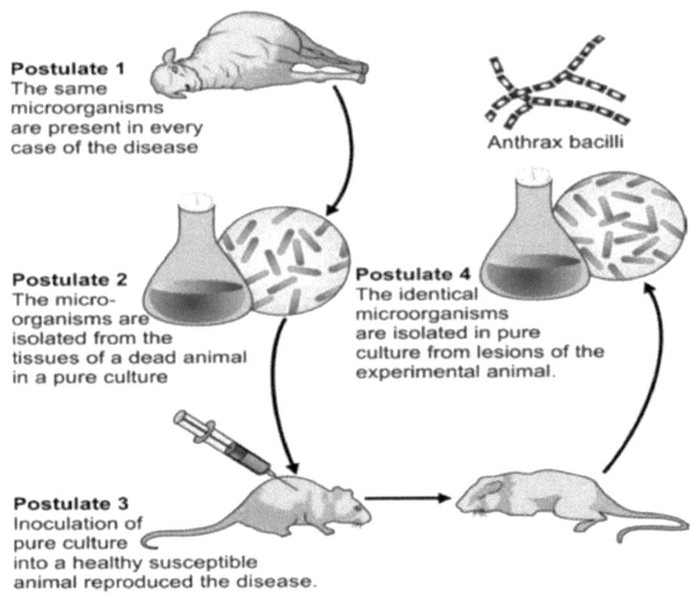

Fig. 1.3: Demonstration of Koch's postulates

Koch postulates

Q 4. Explain in detail about Historical perspectives.

= Microbiology is the study of living organisms of microscopic size.

Microbiology is divided in four era's the are as follows .

1 .DISCOVERY ERA:

"Spontaneous generation" Aristotle (384-322) and others believed that living organisms could develop from non-living materials.

In 13th century, Rogen Bacon described that the disease caused by a minute "seed" or "germ".

Antony Van Leeuwenhoek (1632 – 1723) Descriptions of Protozoa, basic types of bacteria, yeasts and algae. Father of Bacteriology and protozoology. In 1676, he observed and described microorganisms such as bacteria and protozoa as "Animalcules".

2.TRANSITION ERA:

Francesco Redi (1626 - 1697) . He showed that maggots would not arise from decaying meat, when it is covered.

John Needham (1713 – 1781) Supporter of the spontaneous generation theory. He proposed that tiny organism(animalcules) arose spontaneously on the mutton gravy. He covered the flasks with cork as done by Redi, Still the microbes appeared on mutton broth.

Lazzaro spallanzai (1729 – 1799) . He demonstrated that air carried germs to the culture medium.

He showed that boiled broth would not give rise to microscopic forms of life.

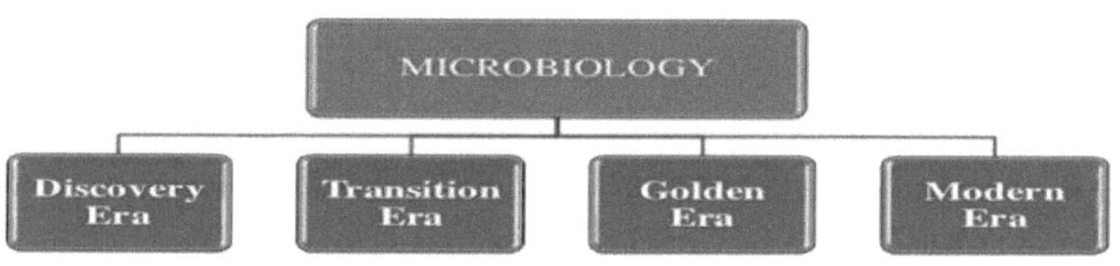

four Era's

3.GOLDEN ERA:

Louis Pasteur : He is the father of Medical Microbiology. He pointed that no growth took place in swan neck shaped tubes because dust and germs had been trapped on the walls of the curved necks but if the necks were broken off so that dust fell directly down into the flask, microbial growth commenced immediately.

Robert Koch (1893-1910) : He demonstrated the role of bacteria in causing disease.

Edward Jenner (1749-1823) : First to prevent small pox. He discovered the technique of vaccination.

Alexander Flemming : He discovered the penicillin from penicillium notatum that destroy several pathogenic bacteria.

4.MODERN ERA:

Modern microbiology. Modern microbiology reaches into many fields of human endeavor, including the development of pharmaceutical products, the use of quality-control methods in food and dairy product production, the control of disease-causing microorganisms in consumable waters, and the industrial applications of microorganisms.

Q 5. Explain the germ theory of disease.

= The germ theory of disease postulated by Pasteur was later further developed by later scientists, such as Robert Koch.

1. The germ theory of disease is the currently accepted scientific theory for many diseases.
2. It states that microorganisms known as pathogens or "germs" can lead to disease.
3. These small organisms, too small to see without magnification, invade humans, other animals, and other living hosts.
4. Their growth and reproduction within their hosts can cause disease.
5. "Germ" may refer to not just a bacterium but to any type of microorganism or even non-living pathogens that can cause disease, such as protists, fungi, viruses, prions, or viroids.
6. Diseases caused by pathogens are called infectious diseases.
7. Even when a pathogen is the principal cause of a disease, environmental and hereditary factors often influence the severity of the disease, and whether a potential host individual becomes infected when exposed to the pathogen.
8. The germ theory of disease postulated by Pasteur was later further developed by later scientists, such as Robert Koch.

CHAPTER TWO

GENERAL CHARACTERISTICS OF MICROBES

Q 1. Draw a neat labelled diagram of Bacterial cell.

=

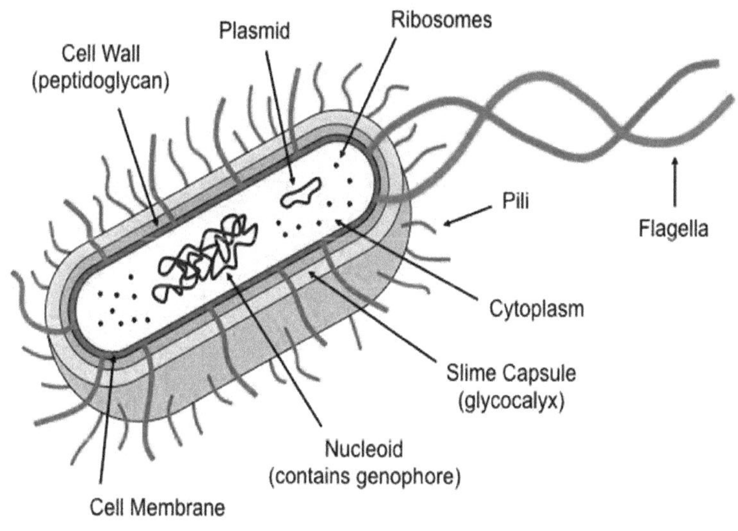

I

Bacterial cell.

Q 2. Differentiate between Gram Positive Bacteria & Gram negative bacteria .

=

S.No	Characteristics	Gram positive Bacteria	Gram negative Bacteria
1.	Cell wall	Single layered with 0.015μm-0.02μm	Triple layered with 0.0075μm–0.012μm thick
2.	Rigidity of cell wall	Rigid due to presence of Peptidoglycans	Elastic due to presence of lipoprotein-polysaccharide mixture
3.	Chemical composition	Peptidoglycans-80% Polysaccharide-20% Teichoic acid present	Peptidoglycans-3 to 12% rest is polysaccharides and lipoproteins. Teichoic acid absent
4.	Outer membrane	Absent	Present
5.	Periplasmic space	Absent	Present
6.	Susceptibility to penicillin	Highly susceptible	Low susceptible
7.	Nutritional requirements	Relatively complex	Relatively simple
8.	Flagella	Contain 2 basal body rings	Contain 4 basal body rings
9.	Lipid and lipoproteins	Low	High
10.	Lipopolysaccharides	Absent	Present

Differentiate between Gram Positive Bacteria & Gram negative bacteria

Q 3. Differentiate between Flagella & Fimbriae.

=

FLAGELLA
VERSUS
PILI

FLAGELLA	PILI
Flagella are helical, but not straight	Pili are non-helical and straight
Long and whip-like	Short and hair-like
Thicker than pili, 15-20 nm in diameter	Thin, 3-10 nm in diameter
Can be either polar, lateral or peritrichous	Occur throughout the surface of the cell
Found in gram positive and gram negative bacteria	Only found in gram negative bacteria
Made up of flagellin protein	Made up of pilin protein
Originate from the cell wall	Originate from the cytoplasmic membrane
Not required for conjugation	Required for conjugation
There are three types: bacterial, archaeal and eukaryotic	There are two types: conjugative and type IV
Mainly responsible for motility	Mainly responsible for attachment during conjugation
Exhibit an undulating, sinusoidal motion	A twitching motility is shown by type IV pili
Occur in *Salmonella*	Occur in *Pseudomonas*

Visit www.pediaa.com

Differentiate between Flagella & Fimbriae.

Q 4. Differentiate between Prokaryotic & Eukaryotic cell.

=

Prokaryotes	Eukaryotes
Circular DNA (in cytosol)	Linear DNA (in nucleus)
No organelles	Several membrane bound organelles
Nucleoid (not membrane bound)	Nucleus (membrane bound)
Single chromosome	Several chromosomes
Plasma membrane typically lacks receptors	Plasma membrane with receptors (sterols and carbohydrates)
Chemically complex cell wall (may contain peptidoglycan)	Chemically simple cell walls (cellulose (plants) and chitin (fungi))
DNA transctription and mRNA translation occurs simultaneously (in cytosol)	DNA transctription in nucleus, and mRNA translation in cytosol
Flagellum (if present) Simple, built from two proteins	Flagellum (if present) Complex, built from microtubules
May have pili and fimbriae	May have cilia
Haploid genome (only one copy of each gene)	Diploid genome (more than one copy of each gene)
May have plasmids (DNA outside chromosome)	Plasmid DNA not common
Compact genome (little repetitive DNA)	Usually large amounts of non-coding and repetitive DNA
May have a glycocalyx cover	Glycocalyx only if no cell wall
Small ribosomes	Large ribosomes in cytosol/nucleus small ribosomes in organelles
No histones in chromosome	DNA "wound" around histones
Lacks cytoskeleton	Cytoskeleton (actin, microtubules)
Mycolaginous capsule	No mycolaginous capsule
Cell size range 0.5–100 µm	Cell size range 10–150 µm
Asexual reproduction (binary fission)	Sexual reproduction (meiosis and mitosis)

Differentiate between Prokaryotic & Eukaryotic cell.

Example : Fungi, protozoa, plants, animals
Eubacteria, All bacteria and blue-green algae

Q 5. Bacterial Growth curve.

= **Bacterial Growth Curve :**

If a suitable liquid medium is inoculated with bacterium and incubated, its growth follows a definitive course. Small samples are taken at regular intervals after inoculation and plotted in relation to time. A plotting of the data will yield a characteristic growth curve . The changes of slope on such a graph indicate the transition from one phase of development to another.

Phases of Bacterial Growth Curve :

The bacterial growth curve can be divided into four major phases:

1. lag phase
2. exponential or log (logarithmic) phase
3. stationary phase, and
4. decline phase.

These phases reflect the physiologic state of the organisms in the culture at that particular time.

1. Lag Phase

After inoculation of the culture medium, multiplication usually does not begin immediately.

The period between inoculation and beginning of multiplication is known as lag phase.

During this period the organisms adapt to the new environment, during which necessary enzymes and intermediate metabolites are built up in adequate quantities for multiplication to proceed.

There is increase in the size of the cells but there is no appreciable increase in numbers.

2. Log (Logarithmic) or Exponential Phase

The cell division starts and their numbers exponentially or by geometric progression with time. If the logarithm of the viable count is plotted against time, a straight line is obtained.

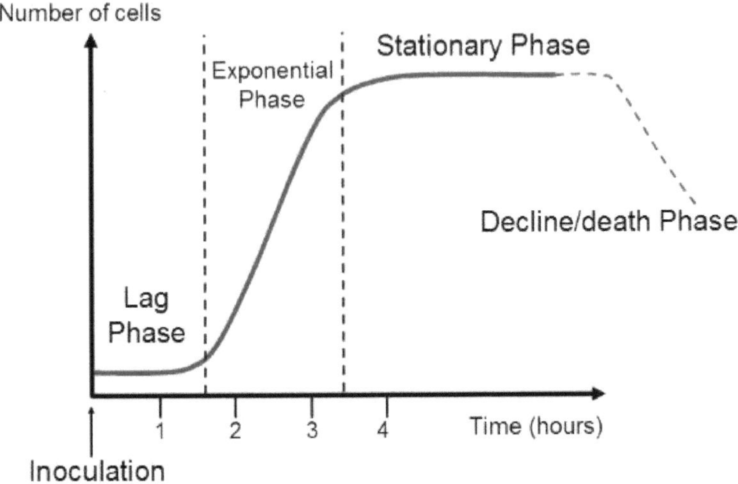

Phases of Bacterial Growth Curve

3. Stationary Phase

After log phase, the bacterial growth ceases almost completely due to exhaustion of nutrients and accumulation of toxic products. The number of progeny cells formed is just enough to replace the number of cells that die. The number of viable cells remain stationary as there is almost a balance between the dying cells and the new formed cells.

4. Phase of Decline

Alter a period of stationary phase, the bacterial population decreases due to the death of cells. The decline phase starts due to exclusion of nutrients, accumulation of toxic produces and autolytic enzymes. There is decline in viable count and not in total count.

Q 6. Gram Staining.

= The technique was developed by a Danish physician . Dr hanes Cristain Gram 1884. This is useful differentialstaining procedure in bacteriology which besides determining gross morphology differentiate **Bacteria into two major distinct groups**:

1) Gram Positive .

2) Gram Negative .

The technique involves six basic steps :

i. Smear preparation
ii. Heat fixing of smear .
iii. Staining with a crystal violet (Primary staining)
iv. Use of iodine.
v. Treatment with acetone alcohol mixture (Decolourizing agent) .
vi. Use of safarin (Colour stain) .

Principale :

The peculiar response toward the staining is related to physical and chemical difference in the cell wall of the two groups of bacteria .

In gram negative bacteria the cell wall is thin multibilayered containing high lipid contents which are readily dissolved by alcohol, resulting in pore formation in the cell wall faciliting the leakage of the crystal violet iodine complex of resulting in discoloration of gram negative bacteria which takes safarin and appears red. On other hand

Cell wall of gram positive bacteria are thick, composed mainly proteins and crossed linked mucopeptides on application of decolorizing agent, dehydration caused resulting in closure of pores of cell wall thereby retaning the CV-I complex and do appear blue or Purple.

Gram Staining Procedure

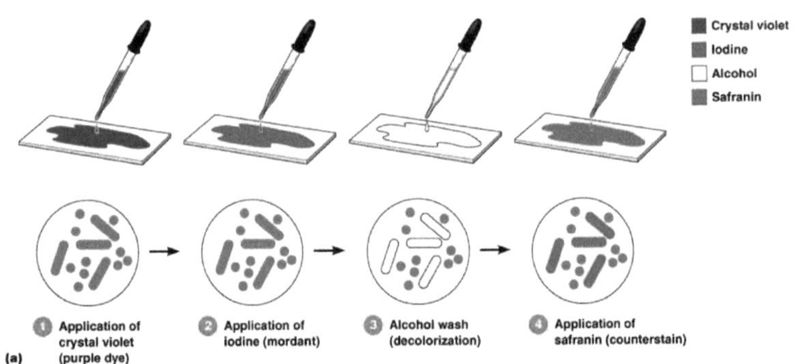

Gram Staining

Reagents Used :

a. Crystal violet
b. Gram iodine solution
c. Ethyl alcohol (15 %) or Alcohol acetone (1:1) solution.
d. Safranin Solution .

Procedure -:

i. Make smear of a given culture on a clear glass slide.
ii. Air dry the smear and heat fix it .
iii. Cover the smear completely with crystal violet stain and leave the stain on the slide for one minute .
iv. Wash the slide gently indistilled water or tap water
v. Flood the spray with gram iodine solution for 1 minute .

vi. Wash with tap water gently and drain care fully .
vii. Wash the slide gently under running water for 30 min .
viii. Now counter stain with safari and wait for 30 min .
ix. Wash again and flot dry with bloting paper or simply air dry the slide and observe under oil. Immersion objective.

Result :

Bacteria that appear blue / violet / purple are assigned as gram positive.

While as those appearning red / pink are assigned as gram negative .

Q 7. Acid fast staining.

= The technique was developed by Paul Ehrlich . and was modified later by Ziehl nelson .

This is a differential staining used to identify mainly the member of mycobacterium especially these organism are difficult to stain by ordinary staining method due to presence of high lipid content in their cell wall .

Bacteria are Classified as :

1. Acid fast : They retain primery stain after the application of strong the application of strong acid and appe red
2. Non Acid fast : if they not retain the primary stain and are counter stained by methylene blue .

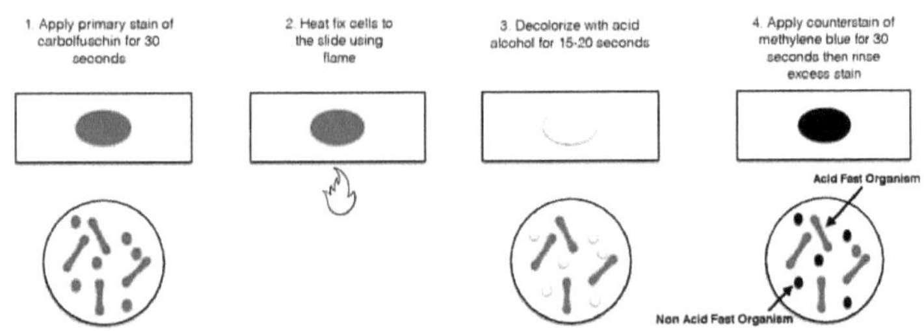

Acid fast staining.

Reagent :

i. Carbol fusion solution .
ii. Acid alchol solution (20 – 25 % v/v in water .)
iii. Methylene blue counter stain (0.3 w/v aqueous)

Procedure :

i. Prepare a smear of purulent portion of the specimen on a clean glass slide
ii. Air dry and heat fix the smear
iii. Flood the smear with freshly filtered carbol Fuchisin. Heat gently until steam rises.
iv. Cool and wash the stain of the slide with H_2o
v. Cover the slide with acid alchol solution for 3 min . Wash with running tap water and drain finally, wash it .
vi. Cover the slide with methylene blue stain and leave it for 2 min .
vii. Wash with tap water, blot dry or air dry the slide andobserve under oil immersion object.

Result : Acid fast organisms will apper bright red on a blue background . While as non acid fast organism will apper dark blue in colour.

Q 8 .Hanging drop method.

= Hanging drop preparation is a special type of wet mount (in which a drop of medium containing the organisms is placed on a microscope slide), often is used in dark illumination to observe the motility of bacteria.

Hanging Drop Method Preparation

In this method, a drop of culture is placed on a coverslip that is encircled with petroleum jelly (or any other sticky material). The coverslip and drop are then inverted over the well of a depression slide. The drop hangs from the coverslip, and the petroleum jelly forms a seal that prevents evaporation. This preparation gives good views of microbial motility.

Materials required

- Glass slides (glass slide with depression) or normal glass slide with adhesive or paraffin ring
- Paraffin wax
- Loop
- Coverslip
- Microscope
- Bunsen burner
- Young broth culture of motile bacteria (e.g. Proteus mirabilis)

Procedure

i. Take a clean glass slide and apply paraffin ring, adhesive tape ring to make circular concavity. (This step is not needed if a glass slide with depression is available).
ii. Hold a clean coverslip by its edges and carefully dab Vaseline on its corners using a toothpick.
iii. Place a loopful of the broth culture to be tested in the centre of the prepared coverslip.

iv. Turn the prepared glass slide or concavity slide upside down (concavity down) over the drop on the coverslip so that the Vaseline seals the coverslip to the slide around the concavity.

v. Turn the slide over so the coverslip is on top and the drop can be observed hanging from the coverslip over the concavity.

vi. Place the preparation in the microscope slide holder and align it using the naked eye so an edge of the drop is under the low power objectives.

vii. Turn the objective to its lowest position using the coarse adjustment and CLOSE THE DIAPHRAGM.

viii. Look through the eyepiece and raise the objective slowly using the coarse adjustment knob until the edge of the drop is observed as an irregular line crossing the field.

ix. Move the slide to make that line (the edge of the drop) pass through the centre of the field.

x. Without raising or lowering the tube, swing the high dry objective into position (Be sure the high dry objective is clean).

xi. Observe the slide through the eyepiece and adjust the fine adjustment until the edge of the drop can be seen as a thick, usually dark line.

xii. Focus the edge of the drop carefully and look at each side of that line for very small objects that are the bacteria. The cells will look either like dark or slightly greenish, very small rods or spheres. Remember the high dry objective magnifies a little less than half as much as the oil immersion objective.

xiii. Adjust the light using the diaphragm lever to maximize the visibility of the cells.

xiv. Observe the cells noting their morphology and grouping and determine whether true motility can be observed.

xv. Brownian movement should be visible on slides of all the organisms, but there should also show true motility.

xvi. Wash the depression slide and after soaking in lysol buckets or discard the prepared glass slide.

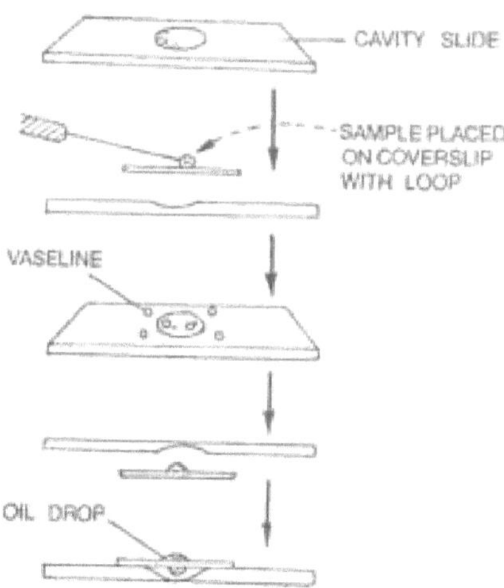

Hanging drop method

Hanging drop slides are useful in observing the general shape of living bacteria and the arrangement of bacterial cells when they associate together. Organisms are observed in a drop that is suspended under a cover glass in a concave depression slide.

Q 9.Bacterial flagella.

= Flagella :

Motile bacteria, except spirochetes, possess one or more unbranched, long, sinuous filaments called flagella, which are the organs of locomotion.

Structure :

They are long, hollow, helical filaments, usually several times the length of the cell. They are 3-20 µm long and are of uniform diameter (0.01-0.013 µm) and terminate in a square tip.

Flagella can be found on both gram-positive and gram-negative bacilli.

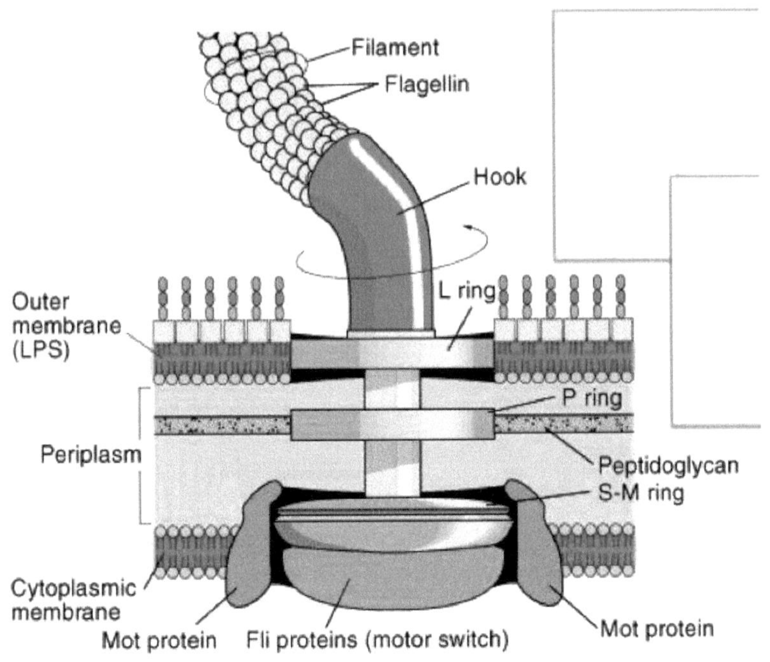

Bacterial flagella.

Parts and Composition :

Each flagellum consists of **three** parts

i. Filament

ii. Hook

iii. Basal body.

i. Filament: The filament is the longest and most Obvious portion which extends from the cell surface to the tip.

ii. Hook: The hook is a short, curved segment which links the filament to its basal body and functions as universal joint between the basal body and the filament.

iii. Basal body: The basal body is embedded in the

cell (cytoplasmic membrane). In the gram-negative bacteria, the basal body has four rings connected to a central rod (L, P, S and M).

Gram-positive bacteria have only two basal

body rings, an inner ring connected to the cytoplasmic membrane and an outer one probably attached

to peptidoglycan.

Arrangement/Types :

The number and location of flagella are distinctive for

each genus. There are four types of flagella arrangement:

- Monotrichous—Single polar flagellum (e.g. Cholera vibrio).
- Amphitrichous—Single flagellum at both ends

(e.g. Alcaligenes faecalis).

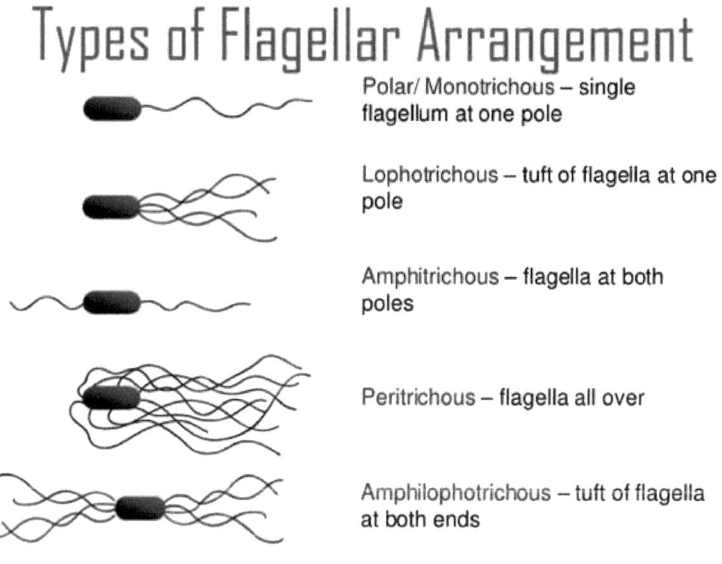

Types of flagella arrangement

- Lophotrichous—Tuft of flagella at one or both ends

(e.g. spirilla).

- Peritrichous—Flagella surrounding the cell (e.g.

Typhoid bacilli).

Flagella are about 0.02 µm in thickness and hence beyond the resolution limit of the light microscope.

Q 10. Bacterial Spore

= **Bacterial Spore ;**

A number of gram-positive bacteria, such as those ofthe genera Clostridium and Bacillus can form a special resistant dormant structure called an endospore or, simply, spores. Endospore develop when essential nutrients are depleted. In sporulation, each vegetative cell forms only one spore, and in subsequent germination, each spore gives rise to a single vegetative cell. Sporulation in bacteria, therefore, is not a method of reproduction but of preservation.

Sporulation : Spore formation, sporogenesis or sporulation normally commences when growth ceases due to lack of nutrients, depletion of the nitrogen or carbon source (or both) being the most significant factor. New antigens appear on sporulation that are not found in the vegetative cell.

Stages:

It is a complex process and may be divided into several stages .

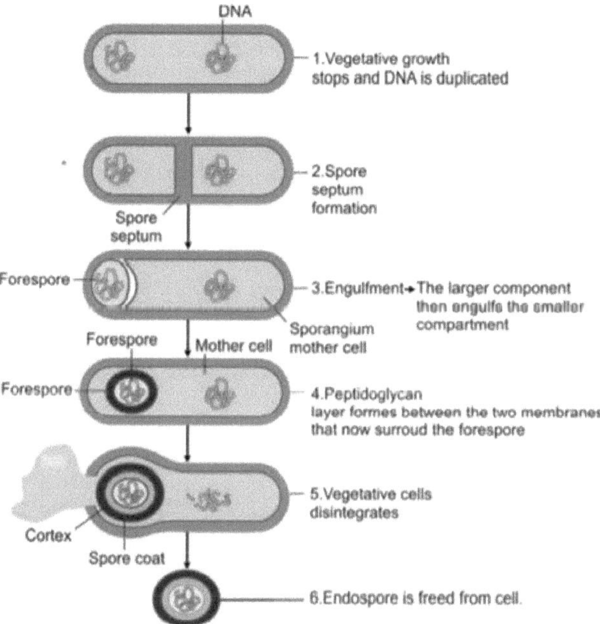

Fig. 3.10: The stages of endospore formation

1 • **Spore septum:** In the first observable stage of sporulation, a newly replicated bacterial chromosome and a small portion of cytoplasm are isolated by an in growth of the plasma membrane called a spore septum.

2 • **Forespore:** The spore septum becomes a doublelayered membrane that surrounds the chromosome and cytoplasm. Structure, entirely enclosed within the original cell, is called a forespore.

3 • **Spore coat:** The forespore is subsequently completely encircled by dividing septum as a double layered membrane. The two spore membranes now engage in active synthesis of various layers of the spore. The inner layer becomes the inner membrane. Between the two layers is laid spore cortex and outer layer is

transformed into spore coat which consists of several layers. In some species from outer layer also develops exosporium which bears ridges and folds .

4 • **Free endospore:** Finally exosporium disintegrates and the endospore is freed.

Q 11. Explain in detail about morphology of bacteria & structural components of bacterial cell along with their function.

= Bacteria are very small in size. The unit of measurement in bacteriology is the micron or micrometer (mm). Bacteria of medical importance generally measure 0.2-1.5 µm in diameter and about 3-5 µm in length. To see bacteria, a light microscope must be used.

Shape of Bacteria Depending on their shape, bacteria are classified into several varieties :

1. Cocci : Cocci (from kokkos meaning berry) are
spherical, or nearly spherical.

2. Bacilli: Bacilli (from baculus meaning rod) are relatively straight, rod shaped (cylindrical) cells. In some of the bacilli, the length of the cells may be equal to width. Such bacillary forms are known as coccobacilli and have to be carefully differentiated from cocci.

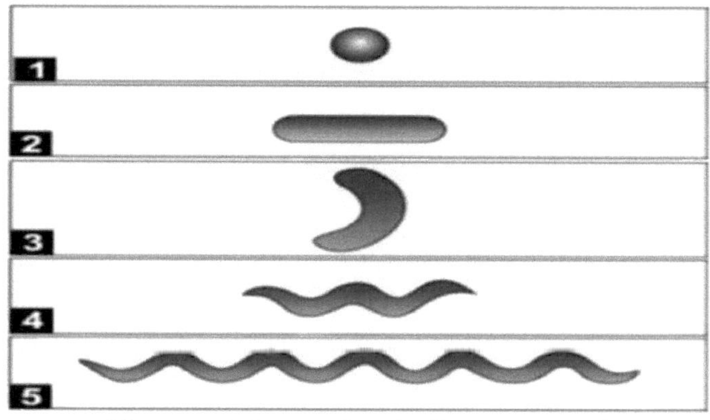

. Shape of bacteria: 1. Coccus; 2. Bacillus; 3. Vibrio; 4. Spirillum; 5. Spirochete

3. Vibrios: Vibrios are curved or comma-shaped rods and derive the name from their characteristic vibratory motility.

4. Spirilla: Spirilla are rigid spiral or helical forms.

5. Spirochetes: Spirochetes (from speira meaning coil and chaite meaning hair) are flexuous spiral forms.

6. Mycoplasma: Mycoplasma are cell wall deficient bacteria and hence do not possess a stable morphology. They occur as round or oval bodies and interlacing filaments.

Cocci Arrangement

i. Diplococci: Cocci may be arranged in pairs (diplococci) when cocci divide and remain together.

ii. Long chains: Long chains (Streptococcus, Enterococcus, and Lactococcus) when cells adhere after repeated divisions in one plane.

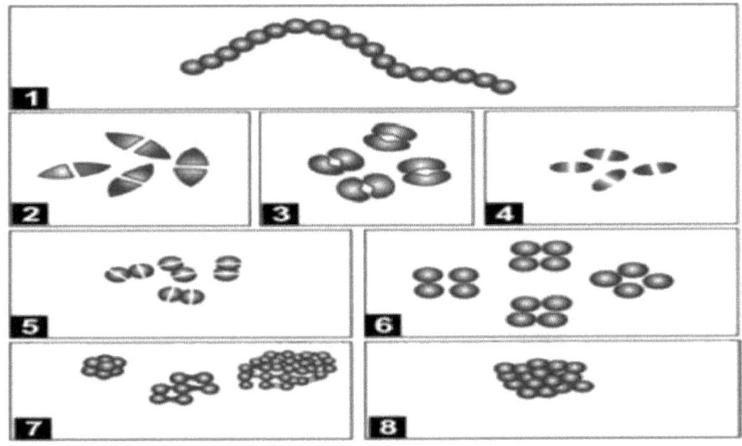

iii. Grape like clusters: Grape like clusters (staphylococci) when cocci divide in random planes.

iv. Tetrads: Square groups of four cells (tetrads) when cocci divide in two planes as in members of the genus Micrococcus.

v. Cubical packets: Cubical packets of eight of cells (genus Sarcina) when cocci divide in three planes.

structural components of bacterial cell

Bacterial Cell Components can be divided into:

a. The outer layer or cell envelope consists of two components:

1. Cell wall.
2. Cytoplasmic or plasma membrane—beneath cell wall.

b. Cellular appendages—Besides these essential components, some bacteria may possess additional structures such as capsule, fimbriae, and flagella.

Capsule: Some bacteria produce a protective gelatinous covering layer called a capsule outside the cell wall. If the capsule is too thin to be seen with light microsope (<0.2 µm) it is called microcapsule.

Loose slime : Soluble, large-molecular, amorphous, viscid colloidal material may be dispersed by the bacterium into the environment as loose slime.

Flagella : Some bacteria carry external filamentous appendages protruding from the cell wall; flagella,which are organs of locomotion; fimbriae, which appear to be organs of adhesion; and pili, which are involved in the transfer of genetic material.

A. Cell envelope and its Appendages

a. The Outer Layer or Cell Envelope

1. Cell Wall

The cell wall is the layer that lies just outside the plasma membrane. It is 10-25 nm thick, strong and relatively rigid, though with some elasticity, and openly porous, being freely permeable to solute molecules smaller than 10 kDa in mass and 1 nm in diameter.

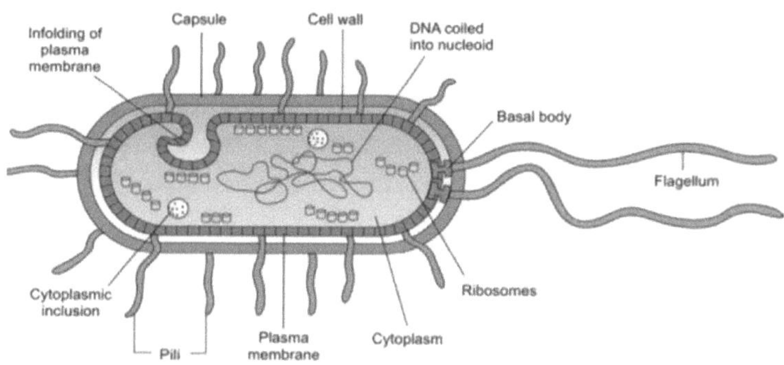

Functions of the cell wall:

1. To impart shape and rigidity to the cell.

2. It supports the weak cytoplasmic membrane against the high internal osmotic pressure of the protoplasm (ranges from 5 and 25 atm).

3. Maintains the characteristic shape of the bacterium.

4. It takes part in cell division.

5. Also functions in interactions (e.g. adhesion) with other bacteria and with mammalian cells.

6. Provide specific protein and carbohydrate receptors for the attachment of some bacterial viruses.

Chemical Structure of Bacterial Cell Wall

chemically the cell wall is composed of mucopeptide (peptidoglycan or murein) scaffolding formed by Nacetyl glucosamine and N-acetyl muramic acid molecules alternating in chains, which are crosslinked by peptide bonds . Peptidoglycan consists of three parts 1. A backbone—composed of alternating N-acetylglucosamine and N-acetylmuramic acid.

2. A set of identical tetrapeptide side chains attached to N-acetylmuramic acid.

3. A set of identical pentapeptide cross-bridges

Q 12Define culture media & classify them on the basis of various methods in detail.

= INTRODUCTION :

Culture medium: A nutrient material prepared for the growth of microorganisms in a laboratory is called a culture medium.

CLASSIFICATION OF MEDIA

Media have been classied into many ways :

A. PHASES OF GROWTH MEDIA ;

Growth media are used in either of the two phases: liquid (broth) or solid (agar) .

1. LIQUID (BROTH) MEDIA

In broth media, nutrients are dissolved in water, and bacterial growth is indicated by a change in broth's appearance from clear to turbid (i.e. cloudy).

Table	Classification of media
A. Based on phases of growth media • 1. Liquid (broth) media • 2. Solid (agar) media • 3. Semisolid media B. Based on nutritional factors • 1. Simple media (basal media) • 2. Complex media • 3. Synthetic or defined media	C. Special media • i. Enriched media • ii. Enrichment media • iii. Selective media • iv. Indicator or differential media • v. Transport media • vi. Sugar media D. Reducing media Based on phases of growth media • 1. Liquid (broth) media • 2. Solid (agar) media • 3. Semisolid media

2. SOLID (AGAR) MEDIA

Solid media are made by adding a solidifying agent to the nutrients and water. Agarose is the most common solidifying agent. The Petri dish containing the agar is referred to as agar.

3. SEMISOLID MEDIA

For special purposes where agar is added to media in concentrations that aretoo low to solidify them.

B. BASED ON NUTRITIONAL FACTORS

1. Simple media (Basal media): Simple media are those which contain only basic nutrients required for the growth of ordinary organisms, and used as a general purpose media, e.g. peptone water, nutrient broth and nutrient agar .

2. Complex media: Media that contain some ingredients of unknown chemical composition are called complex media. One common ingredient is peptone.

Extracts, which are the water-soluble components of a substance, are also used.

SYNTHETIC OR CHEMICALLY DEFINED MEDIA

They are prepared exclusively from pure chemical substances and their exact composition is known.

C. SPECIAL MEDIA

I. ENRICHED MEDIA

These are prepared to meet the nutritional requirements of more exacting

bacteria by the addition of substances such as blood, serum or egg to a basal medium.

EXAMPLES OF ENRICHED MEDIA

1. Blood agar
2. Chocolate agar

III. SELECTIVE MEDIA

When a substance is added to a solid medium which inhibits the growth of unwanted bacteria but favours the growth of wanted bacteria, it is known as selective media. These media are used to isolate particular bacteria from specimens where mixed bacterial flora is expected.

Examples of selective media :

1. Deoxycholate citrate agar (DCA): Addition of deoxycholate acts as a

selective agent for dysentery bacilli (isolation of Shigellae).

2. Lowenstein-Jensen medium : This medium is used for Mycobacterium tuberculosis.

3. Bile salt agar (BSA): Bile salt is a selective agent. It faredurs the growth of only Vibrio cholerae and inhibits the growth of intestinal organisms.

IV. INDICATOR MEDIA

These media contain an indicator which changes colour when a bacterium grows in them.

Examples:

1. Wilson and Blair medium:
2. MacConkey agar

V. DIFFERENTIAL MEDIA

A medium, which has substances incorporated in it, enabling it to bring out

differing characteristics of bacteria and thus helping to distinguish between

them, is called a differential medium.

Example

MacConkey agar : MacConkey agar is both differential and selective.

VI. SUGAR MEDIA

For the identication of most of the organisms, sugar fermentation reactions are carried out. Carbohydrate fermentation is used ‘for characterisation and identication of bacteria, particularly important in the study of Gram-negative bacilli. Sugar media are used to test fermentation.

Sugar used for sugar media: The term ‘sugar’ in microbiology denotes any fermentable substance. Glucose, lactose, sucrose and mannitol are routinely employed for fermentation tests.

VII. TRANSPORT MEDIA

A transport medium is a holding medium designed to preserve the viability of microorganisms in the specimen but not allow multiplication.

Examples

1. Stuart’s transport medium and Amines transport medium for gonococci.

2. Buffered glycerol saline for enteric bacilli.

Q 13. Define & Draw a neat labelled diagram of bacterial spore.

=

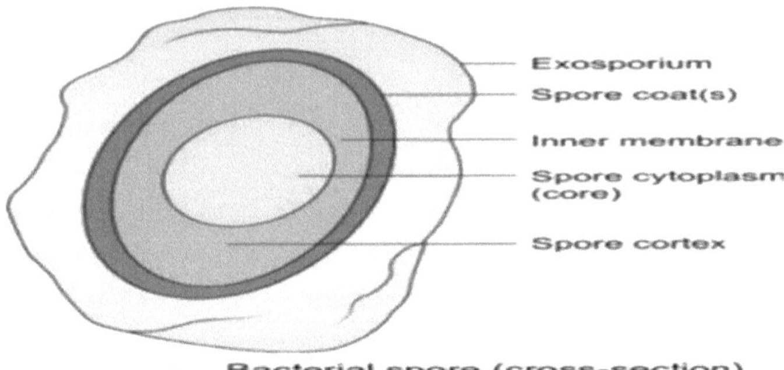

Bacterial spore (cross-section)

Bacterial spores serve largely as a resting, or dormant, stage in the bacterial life cycle, helping to preserve the bacterium through periods of unfavourable conditions. Spore production is particularly common among Bacillus and Clostridium bacteria, several species of which are disease-causing.

CHAPTER THREE

INFECTION CONTROL

Q 1. Sources of infection

= Infection and immunity involve interaction between the animal body (host) and the infecting microorganisms .

The lodgement and multiplication of a parasite in or on the tissues of a host constitute infection. It does not invariably result in disease.

SOURCES OF INFECTION

1. Human beings

2. Animals

3. Insects

4. Soil and water

5. Food.

A. HUMAN BEINGS

The most common source of infection for human beings is human beings themselves. The parasite may originate from a patient or carrier.

Humans serving as the microbial reservoir:

1. Acquisition of "strep" throat through touching

2. Hepatitis by blood transfusions

3. Gonorrhea, syphilis, and AIDS by sexual contact

4. Tuberculosis by coughing; and the common cold through sneezing.

B. ANIMALS

Reservoir hosts: Many pathogens are capable of causing infections in both human beings and animals. Therefore, animals may act as a source of infection of such organisms. These, animals serve to maintain the parasite in nature and act as reservoir and they are, therefore, called reservoir hosts.

Zoonosis: The diseases and infections, which are transmissible to man from animals are called zoonosis.

Examples of zoonotic diseases

Bacterial: Anthrax, brucellosis, Q fever, leptospirosis, bovine tuberculosis, bubonic plague, Salmonella food poisoning.

Viral: Rabies, yellow fever, cowpox, monkeypox.

Protozoal: Leishmaniasis, toxoplasmosis, trypanosomiasis, babesiosis.

Helminthic: Echinococcosis, taeniasis, trichinellosis.

Fungal: Microsporum canis, Trichophyton verrucosum.

C. INSECTS

ARTHROPOD-BORNE DISEASES

Blood-sucking insects, such as mosquitos, ticks, mites, ies, and lice may transmit pathogens to human beings and diseases so caused are called arthropod borne diseases.

VECTORS

Insects that transmit infections are called vectors. Vector-borne transmission

can be of two types either mechanical (external) or biological (internal).

1. Mechanical vector: The disease agent is transmitted mechanically by the arthropod.

Examples: Transmission of diarrhea, dysentery, typhoid, food poisoning and

tracghoma by the housely.

2. Biological vectors: Biological vectors are those in whom the pathogens

multiply suciently or has undergone a developmental cycle. The interval between the time of entry of the pathogen into the vector and the vector

becoming infective is called the extrinsic incubation period.

Examples: Aedes aegypti mosquito in yellow fever, Anopheles mosquito in malaria.

Reservoir hosts: Besides acting as vectors, some insects may also act as

reservoir hosts (for example, ticks in relapsing fever and spotted fever).

Infection is maintained in such insects by transovarial or transstadial passage.

D. SOIL AND WATER

I. SOIL

Some pathogens can survive in the soil for long periods.

Examples

1. Spores of tetanus and gas gangrene: Spores of tetanus and gas gangrene remain viable in the soil for several decades and serve as source of infection.

2. Fungi and parasites: Fungi (causing mycetoma, sporotrichosis, histoplasmosis) and parasites such as roundworms and hookworms also survive in the soil and cause human infection.

II. WATER

Water may act as the source of infection either due to contamination with pathogenic microorganisms (Shigella, Salmonella, Vibrio cholerae, poliomyelitis

virus, hepatitis virus) or due the presence of aquatic vector (cyclops containing larvae of guinea worm infection).

E. FOOD

Contaminated food may act as source of infection of organisms causing food poisoning, gastroenteritits, diarrhea and dysentery.

Q 2. Classification of infection

= The lodgement and multiplication of a parasite in or on the tissues of a host constitute infection. It does not invariably result in disease.

CLASSIFICATION OF INFECTIONS

Infections may be classied in various ways:

1. Primary infection: Initial infection with a parasite in a host is termed primary

infection.

2. Reinfections: Subsequent infections by the same parasite in the host are termed reinfections.

3. Secondary infection: When a new parasite sets up an infection in a host

whose resistance is lowered by a preexisting infectious disease, this is

termed secondary infection.

4. Local infection: The term local infection (more appropriately local sepsis)

indicates a condition where, due to infection or sepsis at localized sites such as appendix or tonsils, generalized effects are produced.

5. Cross-infection: When in a patient already suffering from a disease, a new infection is set up from another host or another external source, it is termed cross-infection.

6. Nosocomial infections: Cross-infections occurring in hospitals are called nosocomial infections (from Greek nosocomion hospital).

7. Iatrogenic infection: The term iatrogenic infection refers to physician induced infections resulting from investigative, therapeutic or other procedures.

8. In apparent infection: In apparent infection is one where clinical effects are not apparent.

9. Subclinical infection: The term subclinical infection is often used as a

synonym to in apparent infection.

10. Atypical infection: Atypical infection is one in which the typical or

characteristic clinical manifestations of the particular infectious disease are not present.

11. Acute infection: An infection which lasts for a relatively short time. (few days to few weeks). E.g. Measles.

12. Chronic infection: An infection which lasts for a long time (over months & years). E.g. TB.

13. Autoinfection: An infection that occurs between two sites on the same host.(worms)

14. Mixed infection: An infection caused by two or more organism.(bacterial vaginosis)

15. Masked infection: An infection is known to occur but the infectious agent cannot be demonstrated.

16. Oppurtunistic infection: An infection with organisms which are normally harmless but become pathogenic when the body's defence mechanisms are compromised.

Q 3. Define carrier & its classification with examples.

= CARRIER

A carrier is person who harbours or lodge of the microorganisms without suffering from any ill effect' because of it. There are several types of carriers:

1. Convalescent carrier: An individual who has recovered from the infectious disease but continues to harbour or lodge large numbers of pathogen.

2. Healthy carrier: A healthy carrier is an individual who harbours or lodge the pathogen but is not ill.

3. Incubatory carrier: An incubatory carrier is an individual who is incubating the pathogen in large numbers but is not yet ill.

4. Temporary carriers: Convalescent, healthy, and incubatory carriers may harbour or lodge the pathogen for only a brief period (hours, days, or weeks) and lasts less than six months.

5. Chronic carriers: They harbour the pathogen for long periods (months, years, or life).

6. Contact carriers: The term contact carrier is applied to a person who acquires the pathogen from a patient.

7. Paradoxical carrier: This refers to a carrier who acquires the pathogens from another carrier.

Q 4. Modes of transmission of infection

= **MODES OF TRANSMISSION OF INFECTION**

Pathogenic organisms can spread from one host to another by a variety of mechanisms. These include as follows:

1. CONTACT

Infection may be acquired by contact, which may be direct or indirect.

1. Direct contact: Diseases transmitted by direct contact include STD (sexually

transmitted diseases), such as syphilis, gonorrhea, lymphogranuloma

venereum, lymphogranuloma inguinale, trichomoniasis, herpes simplex type 2, hepatitis B and acquired immunodeciency syndrome (AIDS).

2. Indirect contact: Fomites: Indirect contact may be through the agency of fomites, which are inanimate objects, such as clothing, pencils or toys which may be contaminated by a pathogen from one person and act as a vehicle for its transmission to another.

2. INHALATION

Droplet nuclei: Respiratory infections, such as common cold, inuenza,

measles, mumps, tuberculosis and whooping cough are acquired by inhalation.

3. INGESTION

Intestinal infections are generally acquired by the ingestion of food or drink

contaminated by pathogens. Infection transmitted by ingestion may be waterborne (cholera), food borne (food poisoning) or handborne (dysentery).

Diseases transmitted by water and food include chiey infections of the

alimentary tract, e.g. acute diarrheas, typhoid fever, cholera, polio, hepatitis A,

food poisoning and intestinal parasites.

4. INOCULATION

The disease agent may be inoculated directly in to the skin or mucosa, e.g.

rabies virus deposited subcutaneously by dog bite, tetanus spores implanted in

deep wounds, and arboviruses injected by insect vectors.

Infection by inoculation may be iatrogenic when unsterile syringes and

surgical equipment are employed. Hepatitis B and the human

immunodeciency virus (HIV).

5. INSECTS

VECTOR-BORNE

Vector is dened as an arthropod or any living carrier (e.g. snail) that transports

an infectious agent to a susceptible individual. In some diseases, blood-sucking insects play an important role in the spread of infection from one individual to another.

6. CONGENITAL

VERTICAL TRANSMISSION

Some pathogens are able to cross the placental barrier and reach the fetus in utero. This is known as vertical transmission.

Examples: So-called TORCH agents (Toxoplasma gondii, rubella virus,

cytomegalovirus and herpes virus), varicella virus, syphilis, hepatitis B,

Coxsackie B and AIDS.

Q 5. Aseptic techniques

= The methods which are used to prevent the access of microorganism during the preparation of parenteral products and their testing are called ' Aseptic Techniques'.

Aseptic techniques are used to reduce the risk of post-procedure infections and to minimize the exposure of health care providers to potentially infectious microorganisms.

Aseptic techniques include practices performed just before, during, or after any invasive procedures.

Good aseptic techniques can only be applied if one knows the possible sources contamination. The various sources of contamination are –

Atmosphere, which is contaminated with dust, droplet and droplet nuclei becomes the breeding ground of microorganism.

The hands are a major means of transmitting infection.

Coughing, sneezing and spitting can cause contamination at a considerable distance.

The cloths which absorb dust particles are also a source of contamination. A handkerchief is the richest source of contamination.

The hair, which is constantly exposed to atmospheric dust is source of contamination. These dust particles are liberated from the hair during brushing and shaking of the head.

The unsterile equipment.

The working surface.

Q 6 Characteristics of an ideal disinfectant

= Disinfectants: Chemicals that kill vegetative bacteria, fungi, viruses & rarely bacterial spores.

1.It should have a wide spectrum of activity.

2.It should have fast action.

3.It should be able to destroy infectious agents in clean as well as dirty condition.

4.It should dissolve easily.
5.It should have high penetration power.
6.It should be non-toxic & non-irritant.
7.It should not stain tissues.
8.It should not have unpleasant odour.

Q 7 Define disinfection. Write down the applications of most commonly used disinfectants.

Or Enumerate any 4 chemical disinfectants.

= **Disinfectants:** Chemicals that kill vegetative bacteria, fungi, viruses & rarely bacterial spores.

The various chemical disinfectants are:

1.Phenol & Related compounds:

Phenol also called carbolic acid is the first chemical agent used as an antiseptic introduced by Lord Joseph Lister (1854).

Phenol causes cell membrane damage & cell lysis.

Phenol(1%) has bactericidal action but it is readily absorbed by skin & mucous membrane & causes toxicity. Thus it has been restricted & has been replaced by chemically related compounds like cresol, chloroxylenol, chlorohexidine which are widely used as antiseptics.

Cresol: It is used as a solution of cresol in soaps(Lysol).It is used for disinfection of infected glass ware. In laboratory disinfection of excreta, cleaning floors of wards & operation theatres.

Chloroxylenol: It is active ingredient of Dettol.

Chlorohexidine: It is bactericidal at high dilution. It is an active ingredient of Savlon which is widely used in burns, wounds, pre-operative disinfection of skin, etc.

2.HALOGENS:

Chloride & Iodine are used as disinfectants being strong oxidizing agents.

Iodine:

-Used as skin disinfectant in the forms of iodophores.

-Tincture of iodine (1-2% iodine in 70% alcohol) is used for cleaning or disinfecting skin & treating skin injuries.

-It is virucidal, ameobicidal & active against Tubercle bacilli.

Chlorine:

-Used widely as water disinfectant(0.5 to 1.0 milligram per liter of water is effective).

-Products containing calcium hypochlorite are used for sanitizing utensils in restaurants.

-Sodium hypochlorite is used as disinfectant for laboratory gloves, linen , syringes & reagent bottles.

3.ALDEHYDES:

Two aldehydes are of considerable importance:

Formaldehyde:

-It is bactericidal, sporicidal & virucidal.

-It can be used in gaseous form or an aqueous solution.

-The gaseous form of formaldehyde is used for disinfection of rooms & for fumigation of operation theatres.

-A 10% solution of formalin (Formaldehyde gas + methanol) is used for killing bacterial cultures & suspension, cleaning contaminated surfaces, metal instruments & preservation of tissues for histopathological examination.

-It is also used to sterilize bacterial vaccines & in preparation of toxoid from toxin.

Gluteraldehyde:

-It is more effective & less irritant (toxic) than formaldehyde.

-It is active against bacteria (especially tubercle bacilli)& their spores, fungi & various types of viruses including HIV & Enteroviruses.

-Glidex(2% buffered solution) is a commercial preparation used to sterilize cystoscopes, bronchoscopes, rubber anesthetic tubes, thermometers, polythene tubing, etc.

4.ALCOHOLS:

Pure alcohol has no disinfecting property.

Three kinds of alcohols used as disinfectants are:

Ethyl alcohol(ethanol): EA in concentration between 50-70% is effective against viruses.

Methyl alcohol(methanol): Effective against fungal spores but it is toxic to eyes. Used for treating cabinets & incubators affected by spores.

Isopropyl alcohol(50-70%): Better than ethyl alcohol in bactericidal property used for disinfection of clinical thermometers.

5.DYES:

Two groups of dyes (aniline dyes & acridines) have been extensively used as skin & wound antiseptics. Both these groups are bacteriostatic in high dilution but have low bactericidal activity.

Aniline dyes: Includes malachite green, brilliant green & crystal violet. They are used on skin & mucous membrane as antiseptics & have been also used for some fungal infections like oral thrush.

Acridine dyes: Includes acriflavine , proflavine ,aminacrine & euflavine. They are bacteriostatic & used for treating wounds & for irrigation of bladder & vagina.

Q8. Standard safety measures.

= **Definition:**

Standard safety measures or standard precautions or universal precautions are simple set of effective practices designed to protect health workers and patients from infection with a range of blood borne & other pathogens from both recognized & unrecognized sources. These practices are used when caring for all patients regardless of diagnosis.

These rules are:

1.Single-use disposable injection equipment.

2.Discard contaminated sharps immediately in puncture or leak proof containers.

3.Do not recap needle or use one hand technique for recapping.

4.Do not wash or disinfect latex gloves.

5.Handle soiled linen correctly(cleaning with detergent &hot water).

6.Disinfect instruments & surface areas.

7.Hand hygiene/Hand washing: Hand hygiene is a major component of standard precautions & one of the most effective methods to prevent transmission of pathogens associated with health care.

Technique:1.Hand washing(40-60sec): Wet hands & apply soap; rub all surfaces; rinse hands & dry thoroughly with a single use towel; use towel to turn off faucet.

2.Hand rubbing(20-30sec): Apply enough product to cover all areas of the hands; rub hands until dry.

Hand washing should be done;

●Before & after any direct patient contact & between patients, whether or not gloves are worn.

●Immediately after gloves are removed.

●Before handling an invasive device.

●After touching blood, body fluids, secretion, excretions, non-intact skin, & contaminated items, even if gloves are worn.

●During patient care, when moving from a contaminated to a clean body site of the patient.

●After contact with inanimate objects in the immediate vicinity of the patient.

8.Wear Protective barriers:

●Gloves:

▪Wear when touching blood, body fluids, secretions,excretions,mucus membranes, nonintact skin.

▪Change between tasks & procedures on the same patient after contact with potentially infectious material.

▪Remove after use, before touching non-contaminated items and surfaces,& before going to another patient. Perform hand hygiene immediately after removal.

8.Wear Protective barriers:

●Gloves:

▪Wear when touching blood, body fluids, secretions,excretions,mucus membranes, nonintact skin.

▪Change between tasks & procedures on the same patient after contact with potentially infectious material.

▪Remove after use, before touching non-contaminated items and surfaces,& before going to another patient. Perform hand hygiene immediately after removal.

9.Prevention of needle stick &injuries from other sharp instruments:

Use care when:

▪Handling needles, scalpels,& other sharp instruments or devices.

▪Cleaning used instruments.

▪Disposing of used needles & other sharp instruments.

10.Respiratory hygiene & cough etiquette:

Persons with respiratory symptoms should apply source control measures:

▪Cover their nose & mouth when coughing/ sneezing with tissue or mask, disposal of used tissues & masks, & perform hand hygiene after contact with respiratory secretions.

11.Enviromental cleaning:

▪Use adequate procedures for the routine cleaning &disinfection of environmental & other frequently touched surfaces.

12.Linens:

Handle, transport,& process used linen in a manner which:

▪Prevents skin &mucus membrane exposures & contamination of clothing.

▪Avoid transfer of pathogens to other patients & or the environ

14.Waste disposal:

Ensure safe waste management.

Treat waste contaminated with blood, body fluids, secretions& excretions as clinical waste, in accordance with local regulations.

Human tissues & laboratory waste that is directly associated with specimen processing should also be treated as clinical waste.

Discard single use items properly.

Q 9. Define sterilisation. Describe in detail about sterilisation by heat .

= Sterilization: Sterilization is a process by which an article, surface or medium is freed of all living microorganisms including viruses, bacteria ,their spores & fungi.

Sterile: Material is heated in such a way that it contains no living organisms is said to be sterile.

1. Physical methods:

a. Sunlight

b. Drying

c. Heat: i. Dry heat: Red heat, Flaming, Incineration, Hot air oven.

ii. Moist heat: Temperature below 100°C,

Temperature at 100°C

Temperature above 100°C

d. Filtration

e. Radiation

f. Sonic & Ultra sonic vibrations.

: I. Physical methods

1.SUNLIGHT:

Direct sunlight has sterilizing effect due to combined effect of UV rays & heat rays.

It has bactericidal effect & is one of the natural methods of sterilization of water in rivers , lakes & tanks.

It is used to sterilize blankets, beddings, clothes, utensils, bedpans, etc.

It is experimentally proved that typhoid bacilli when exposed to the sun on piece of white drill cloth were killed in two hours, whereas bacteria remain alive in dark even after six days.

2.DRYING OR DESICCATION:

Moisture is essential for the growth of bacteria, so drying in air has deleterious effect on many bacteria.

However spores are unaffected & can remain alive for several month or even years.

Therefore, it is not an ideal method of sterilization

3.HEAT

Most common and one of the most effective methods of sterilization. Factors influencing sterilization by heat are : -

i. Nature of heat

a. Dry

b. Moist

ii. Temperature & time

iii. No. of organism present

iv. Characteristics of organism such as species& sporing capacity.

v. Type of material from which organism is to be eradicated

1. DRY HEAT:

Dry heat kills microorganisms by causing destructive oxidation of essential cell constituents. The various methods of dry heat sterilization include:

a) Red Heat: It is used to sterilize metallic objects by holding them on flame of Bunsen burner till they are red hot. Example : inoculating wires, needles, forceps & spatulas, etc.

b) Flaming: The article is passed over flame of Bunsen burner for few(3-4) times without allowing it to become red hot or stand too long. Example : Glass slides, mouth of culture tubes &bottles, cover slips, scalpels, blades &needles.

c)Incineration:

It is the process of complete burning of disposable wastes & some biomedical wastes in an electric furnace known as "Incinerator".

It is the best method to decontaminate the destroying material & disposal of biochemical wastes.

It is useful in disposal of:

Soiled dressings, swabs.

Soiled paper & mouth wipes.

Animal carcasses.

Human anatomical waste.

Pathogenic materials.

d)Hot air oven :

Construction:

The hot air oven is made up of double walled steel chamber with stout door.

The top or side contain ventilator which is left open during sterilization, to disperse any moisture.

Air circulates within the oven by convention currents.

This is most widely used method of sterilization by dry heat.

2. Moist heat:

Sterilization by moist heat implies killing microorganisms by steam or hot water. Moist heat kills microorganisms by denaturation and coagulation of proteins. Moist heat in sterilization has 3 temperature ranges:

A. Temperature below 100°C

B. Temperature at 100°C

C. Temperature above 100°C

5. FILTRATION

This method is used for sterilization of liquid substances or fluids such as sera &solutions of heat liable substances such as sugars, urea, enzyme, & antibiotics which get damaged by heat process.

The method is also used for separation of bacteriophages & bacterial toxins from bacteria. The spore size is not less than 0.75m in diameter & it retains bacteria but allows viruses to pass through filtrate. Therefore filtered preparations are not safe & cannot be employed for clinical use.

6.IRRADIATION

Radiation used for sterilization is of two types

Ionizing radiation, e.g., X-rays, gamma rays, and high speed electrons .

Non-ionizing radiation, e.g. ultraviolet light, and infrared light.

These forms of radiation can be used to kill or inactivate microorganisms.

Q 10.Describe the principle of an autoclave.

= **AUTOCLAVE :**

"An autoclave is a modified pressure cooker in which sterilization by saturated steam under high pressure is achieved (autoclaving)".

An autoclave may be horizontal or vertical.

It is a double walled or jacketed chamber (outer chamber) made up of stainless steel or gun metal with supporting frame.

The steam circulates within the jacket and is supplied under high pressure to closed inner chamber where articles for sterilization are kept.

One fifth of the cylinder is filled with water, materials to be sterilized are kept inside, lid closed &heater is put on.

Safety valve is adjusted to required pressure (15psi/inch square).

The boiling of water inside the chamber after sometime results in steam which is allowed to escape with air mixture till the cylinder becomes air free.

The discharge tap is closed & the desired pressure inside in chamber is allowed to rise to the one chosen for autoclaving for a fixed time & thus complete sterilization achieved.

One fifth of the cylinder is filled with water, materials to be sterilized are kept inside, lid closed &heater is put on.

Safety valve is adjusted to required pressure (15psi/inch square).

The boiling of water inside the chamber after sometime results in steam which is allowed to escape with air mixture till the cylinder becomes air free.

The discharge tap is closed & the desired pressure inside in chamber is allowed to rise to the one chosen for autoclaving for a fixed time & thus complete sterilization achieved.

Satisfactory autoclaving or sterilization can be achieved at 15 pounds per square inch(psi) pressure which is equivalent to 121°C of temperature & the time of operation is 15-20 min.

At this temperature most of the heat resistant spores are killed which cannot be achieved by other sterilization methods.

However, sterilization can also be done at higher temperatures, at 126°C(20lbs pressure/inch square) for 10 min or at 133°C(30 lbs pressure/inch2) for 3 min.

Autoclaving is ideal method of destruction of bacterial spores.

It is used to sterilize culture media, rubber goods, syringes, gowns, dressing, linen, gloves, etc.

Q 11.Categories of Biomedical waste.

= DEFINITION:

Biomedical waste means any solid or liquid waste which is generated during the diagnosis, treatment or immunization of human beings or animals, in research activities or in the production or testing of biological products.

Categories of Bio-medical Waste

Schedule-I

Category	Waste Type	Treatment and Disposal Method
Category 1	Human Anatomical Wastes (Tissues, organs, body parts)	Incineration / deep burial
Category 2	Animal Waste	Incineration / deep burial
Category 3	Microbiology and Biotechnology waste	Autoclave/microwave/incineration
Category 4	Sharps	Disinfection (chemical treatment)+/autoclaving/microwaving and mutilation shredding
Category 5	Discarded Medicines and Cytotoxic Drugs	Incineration/ destruction and drugs disposal in secured landfills
Category 6	Contaminated solid waste	Incineration/autoclaving / microwaving
Category 7	Solid waste (disposable items other than sharps)	Disinfection by chemical treatment+ microwaving/autoclaving & mutilation shredding
Category 8	Liquid waste (generated from laboratory washing, cleaning, housekeeping and disinfecting activity)	Disinfection by chemical treatment+ and discharge into the drains
Category 9	Incineration ash	Disposal in municipal landfill
Category10	Chemical Wastes	Chemical Treatment + and discharge in to drain for liquids and secured landfill

Categories of Biomedical waste.

Q 12. Disposal of Biomedical waste.

= **DEFINITION**:

Biomedical waste means any solid or liquid waste which is generated during the diagnosis, treatment or immunization of human beings or animals, in research activities or in the production or testing of biological products.

Different methods of treatment & disposal are;

1.Incineration = Incineration is a method of treating waste which involves the combustion of the organic substances found in waste materials . The key difference between combustion and incineration is that combustion includes the reaction between substances and oxygen, which produces energy, whereas incineration is the destruction of something via burning. ... However, incineration gives ash, flue gas and heat as the final product.

Three types of waste to which incineration is applied extensively are municipal solid waste, hazardous waste, and medical waste. Incineration of those three types is the focus of this discussion.

2.Autoclave = An autoclave is a machine that uses steam under pressure to kill harmful bacteria, viruses, fungi, and spores on items that are placed inside a pressure vessel. The items are heated to an appropriate sterilization temperature for a given amount of time.

An autoclave is used to sterilize surgical equipment, laboratory instruments, pharmaceutical items, and other materials. It can sterilize solids, liquids, hollows, and instruments of various shapes and sizes.

3.Microwave irradiation = Microwave irradiation involves electromagnetic wave in the range of 300 MHz–300 GHz. Typical microwave ovens or microwave reactors work at a frequency of 2.45 GHz. The microwave irradiation produces efficient internal heating by direct coupling of microwave energy with the molecules of biomass.

4.Inertization = Inertization, or inerting, is an explosion protection process that uses inert gas to prevent the formation of an explosive mixture. Inerting systems are used to prevent: vapors from escaping into the atmosphere (contamination) air from penetrating into the plant (oxidation).

inert gases are non-combustible, non-flammable, and non-reactive to many materials. Examples include argon, helium, nitrogen, and neon. ... Some inert gases are also cryogenic in their liquid state.

5.Chemical Disinfection = Chemical disinfection consists of adding a disinfectant (generally a strong oxidant) to the water, which reacts with the organic matter and microbial organisms.

Most frequent chemical disinfection compounds are chlorine dioxide, chlorine, and chloramines on one hand and ozone on the other hand. These include alcohols, chlorine and chlorine compounds, formaldehyde, glutaraldehyde, ortho-phthalaldehyde, hydrogen peroxide, iodophors, peracetic acid, phenolics, and quaternary ammonium compounds.

6.Land Disposal = Definition. The discharge, deposit or injection of any waste onto or into the soil or other land surfaces.

Landfills are sites designated for dumping rubbish, garbage, or other sorts of solid wastes. Historically, they are the most common means of disposing solid waste which is either buried or left to pile in heaps. ... Some landfills are well managed and designed as part of integrated waste management.

Q 13 . What is nosocomial infection. Describe various types of nosocomial infections in detail .

= Hospital-acquired infection (HAI)/nosocomial infection — is an infection that is contracted from the environment or staff of a healthcare facility.

- The term Nosocomial is taken from the Greek word **Nosocomium** meaning healthcare facility.
- It is also known as hospital acquired infection.
- Nosocomial infection is one that is acquired in hospital or health care agency.
- Hospital is one of the most likely places for acquiring and infection because it harbors high population of viral and strains of microorganisms that are usually resistant to do antibiotics.

Types of hospital acquired infection

- **Bloodstream infection** -this include bacteria and septicemia they are generally caused by introduction of intravascular catheter cannulas.

- **Pneumonia -ventilator associated pneumonia(VAP)** in ICU patient patients with prior respiratory tract pathology smokers patient who have undergone abdominal of thoracic surgery are usually affected.
- **Urinary tract infection** it is usually caused by introduction of eggs in organisms urinary tract catheter for urinary tract instrumentation.
- **Gastrointestinal infection** it can occur by consumption of contaminated food and cause food poisoning manifested by vomiting diarrhea or dysentery.
- **Skin and soft tissue infection** it can occurred by surgical procedure and contamination of wound and secondary infection of traumatic wound example of positive microorganisms

Q 13. Define hospital acquired infection. Write a note on hospital infection control committee / program .

= Hospital-acquired infection (HAI)/nosocomial infection — is an infection that is contracted from the environment or staff of a healthcare facility.

- The term Nosocomial is taken from the Greek word **Nosocomium** meaning healthcare facility.
- It is also known as hospital acquired infection.
- Nosocomial infection is one that is acquired in hospital or health care agency.

This committee bears the responsibility of infection control measures with an

objective of reducing the risk of HAI in the hospital. The committee discuss and

decides on each matter that can have an effect on infection control.

Roles and responsibilities

• Develop and approve organization wide infection control programme,

policies, activities and manual

• Establish standard precaution practices to be followed across the hospital

• Establish definitions and criteria for identifying and reporting of all

infections among patients and personnel

• Guide departments on evidence based infection control practices

• Set benchmark HAI rates for monitoring the effectiveness of infection

control measures

• Validate methods for calculating HAI rates

• Review HAI rates periodically and recommend actions accordingly

• Develop antibiotic policy in conjunction with pharmaco-therapeutics

committee

• Develop protocol for handling of infection outbreak and manage such

situations

• Other similar matters related to infection control

Suggested members

? **Chairperson** – Someone from top management such as CEO, Vice president

or director or Medical Superintendent .

? **Convener/Coordinator** – Infection Control Officer / Medical Microbiologist

/ Infectious diseases specialist

? **Clinical members** – One representative each from all clinical specialties and

super-specialties, including Anesthesiology, Critical Care, Emergency

Medicine, Laboratory services, Blood Bank, Nursing Services and Allied

health specialties

Non-clinical members – Person in-charge for administration of Operation

theatre, ICU, IPD, OPD, Emergency department, CSSD, Laundry, Bio-medical

waste, Maintenance, Medical Equipment and General Management

Q 14 . Write down the various sources & routes / modes of transmission of infection.

= **Sources of Infection**

- **Endogenous:**

§ Patients own flora may invade patient's tissue during some surgical

operations or instrumental manipulations

§ Normal commensals of the skin, respiratory, GI, UG tract

- **Exogenous:**

§ From another patient / staff member / environment in the hospital

§ Environmental sources: Inanimate objects, air, water, food

§ Cross infection from: other patients, hospital staff (suffering from

infections or asymptomatic carriers)

Modes of Transmission :

- **1. Contact:**

Most common route of transmission

— **Hands or Clothing:**
- Hands of staff: important vehicle of spread
- Contact of hands & clothing of attendants

Eg: *Staphylococcus aureus, Streptococcus pyrogenes*

— **Inanimate objects:**
- Improper disinfection of Instruments: endoscope, bronchoscope, cystoscope

Eg: *Pseudomonas aeruginosa*

- **2. Airborne:**

— **Droplets:**
- Droplets of Respiratory infections: transmitted by inhalation

— **Dust:**
- Dust from bedding, floors, wound exudates & skin

Eg: *Pseudomonas aeruginosa, Staphylococcus aureus*

— Aerosols:
- Aerosols from nebulizers, humidifiers & AC

Eg: *Legionella pneumophila*

- **3.Oral Route:**

- Hospital food may contain Antibiotic-resistant bacteria → may colonize intestine → can cause infections

- **4. Parenteral route:**

- Disposable syringes & needles
- Certain infections may be transmitted by blood transfusion, tissue donation, contaminated blood products Eg: Hepatitis B, HIV

Q 15. Explain in detail the portals of entry & exit of microorganisms.

= PORTALS OF ENTRY (ENTRY OF MICROBES INTO BODY):

To cause any infection, pathogens must enter the body through certain pathways or routes called portals of entry which differs for various organisms. Most of the pathogens can cause infection only if they enter through a particular route. The portals of entry may be:

1. Alimentary tract: This tract serves as a portal of entry of the pathogenes causing typhoid, dysentry, cholera. These pathogens are taken to alimentary tract via ingestion of contaminated milk, food or water through mouth.

2. Respiratory tract: This tract is a portal of entry of pathogens causing diphtheria, TB, pneumonia, etc. These pathogenes have special affinity for respiratory tract & enter via inhalation or through mucous membrane of mouth, nose to throat, tonsils & lungs.

3. Urogenital tract: Some pathogens enter the body by coming in contact with urogenital tract & are important cause of STD. e.g. pathogens causing AIDS, gonnorhoea, syphilis.

4. Inoculation: Some pathogens enter the body through the skin or mucous membrane through abrasions, wounds or burns & cause severe wound infection. E.g. spores of Cl.tetani enter the wound causing tetanus, Hep.B transmitted by transfusion of contaminated blood or inoculation of infected blood products.

B.) PORTALS OF EXIT (EXIT OF MICROBES FROM BODY):

The pathogens exit from the body of an infected person or carrier through certain routes or pathways called portals of exit. The portals exist differ for different microorganisms depending upon the site or location of infection. The portal of exit may be:

Feces

Urine

Sputum/saliva

Skin & mucous membrane (secretion)

Nose & throat secretions

Eye secretions

Blood

Q 16What is asepsis. Write a detailed note on aseptic techniques.

= *DEFINITION:*

Asepsis is the state of being free from disease causing contaminants such as bacteria, viruses, fungi & parasites or, preventing contact with microorganisms. There are two types of asepsis.

Medical asepsis, also known as **"clean technique"** is aimed at controlling the number of microorganisms and is used for all clinical patient care activities. **Surgical asepsis,** also known as "**sterile technique**" is aimed at removing all microorganisms and is used for all surgical/sterile procedures.

1. **medical asepsis.** = Medical asepsis is the state of being free from disease causing microorganisms. Medical asepsis is concerned with eliminating the spread of microorganisms through facility practices. So cleaning up spills, dirty surfaces and using disinfectant would be examples of this. Medical asepsis also includes the use of PPE (personal protective equipment), like gloves, gowns, and even masks, eye and face shields.
2. **surgical asepsis.** = Surgical asepsis is the absence of all microorganisms within any type of invasive procedure. Sterile technique is a set of specific practices and procedures performed to make equipment and areas free from all microorganisms and to maintain that sterility. The goal of asepsis is to prevent the contamination of the open surgical wound by isolating the operative site from the surrounding nonsterile environment.

Aseptic technique means using practices and procedures to prevent contamination from pathogens. It involves applying the strictest rules to minimize the risk of infection. Healthcare workers use aseptic technique in surgery rooms, clinics, outpatient care centers, and other health care settings.

Following aseptic technique helps prevent the spread of pathogens that cause infection.

Healthcare professionals commonly use aseptic technique when they're:

handling surgery equipment
helping with a baby's birth by vaginal delivery
handling dialysis catheters
performing dialysis
inserting a chest tube
inserting a urinary catheter
inserting central intravenous (IV) or arterial lines
inserting other draining devices
performing various surgical techniques

Aseptic technique benefits

Whenever your skin is opened, you're vulnerable to infection. That's why it's critical for you to get prompt treatment for burns and wounds. Even intentional cuts during surgery put you at risk for infection. The way healthcare providers use aseptic techniques before, during, and after your procedure help protect you from infection.

When you need surgery or other procedures that require aseptic technique, you're already vulnerable to infections. You need your immune system to be at its strongest to heal. You have a better chance of a recovery if you don't have to fight off an infection.

Q17. Write a note on biomedical waste & its management.

= Biomedical waste or hospital waste is any kind of waste containing infectious (or potentially infectious) materials. ... Waste sharps include potentially contaminated used (and unused discarded) needles, scalpels, lancets and other devices capable of penetrating skin.

It may also include waste associated with the generation of biomedical waste that visually appears to be of medical or laboratory origin (e.g. packaging, unused bandages, infusion kits etc.), as well research laboratory waste containing biomolecules or organisms that are mainly restricted from environmental release.

Biomedical waste is generated from biological and medical sources and activities, such as the diagnosis, prevention, or treatment of diseases. Common generators (or producers) of biomedical waste include hospitals, health clinics, nursing homes, emergency medical services, medical research laboratories, offices of physicians, dentists, veterinarians, home health care and morgues or funeral homes. In healthcare facilities (i.e. hospitals, clinics, doctor's offices, veterinary hospitals and clinical laboratories), waste with these characteristics may alternatively be called medical or clinical waste.

Management

Biomedical waste must be properly managed and disposed of to protect the environment, general public and workers, especially healthcare and sanitation workers who are at risk of exposure to biomedical waste as an occupational hazard. Steps in the management of biomedical waste include generation, accumulation, handling, storage, treatment, transport and disposal.

Accumulation, handling, storage ;

Biomedical waste is generated from various sources . it is accumulated on that areas . So source identification is done on that site called segregartion of the area . handling all waste carefully . And store for few hours till the transport vehicle comes to collect it .Store in safe area.

Treatment , Disposal

The goals of biomedical waste treatment are to reduce or eliminate the waste's hazards, and usually to make the waste unrecognizable. Treatment should render the waste safe for subsequent handling and disposal. There are several treatment methods that can accomplish these goals.It include secregating the bio waste

Biomedical waste is often incinerated. An efficient incinerator will destroy pathogens and sharps. Source materials are not recognizable in the resulting ash. Alternative thermal treatment can also include technologies such as gasification[8] and pyrolysis including energy recovery with similar waste volume reductions and pathogen destruction.

An autoclave may also be used to treat biomedical waste. An autoclave uses steam and pressure to sterilize the waste or reduce its microbiological load to a level at which it may be safely disposed of. Many healthcare facilities routinely use an autoclave to sterilize medical supplies. If the same autoclave is used to sterilize supplies and treat biomedical waste, administrative controls must be used to prevent the waste operations from contaminating the supplies. Effective administrative controls include operator training, strict procedures, and separate times and space for processing biomedical waste.

Microwave disinfection can also be employed for treatment of Biomedical wastes.

Or By Volume reduction processess .

Q 18. Sources of infection

= Infection and immunity involve interaction between the animal body (host) and the infecting microorganisms .

The lodgement and multiplication of a parasite in or on the tissues of a host constitute infection. It does not invariably result in disease.

SOURCES OF INFECTION

1. Human beings

2. Animals

3. Insects

4. Soil and water

5. Food.

A. HUMAN BEINGS

The most common source of infection for human beings is human beings themselves. The parasite may originate from a patient or carrier.

Humans serving as the microbial reservoir:

1. Acquisition of “strep” throat through touching
2. Hepatitis by blood transfusions
3. Gonorrhea, syphilis, and AIDS by sexual contact
4. Tuberculosis by coughing; and the common cold through sneezing.

B. ANIMALS

Reservoir hosts: Many pathogens are capable of causing infections in both human beings and animals. Therefore, animals may act as a source of infection of such organisms. These, animals serve to maintain the parasite in nature and act as reservoir and they are, therefore, called reservoir hosts.

Zoonosis: The diseases and infections, which are transmissible to man from animals are called zoonosis.

Examples of zoonotic diseases

Bacterial: Anthrax, brucellosis, Q fever, leptospirosis, bovine tuberculosis, bubonic plague, Salmonella food poisoning.

Viral: Rabies, yellow fever, cowpox, monkeypox.

Protozoal: Leishmaniasis, toxoplasmosis, trypanosomiasis, babesiosis.

Helminthic: Echinococcosis, taeniasis, trichinellosis.

Fungal: Microsporum canis, Trichophyton verrucosum.

C. INSECTS

ARTHROPOD-BORNE DISEASES

Blood-sucking insects, such as mosquitos, ticks, mites, ies, and lice may

transmit pathogens to human beings and diseases so caused are called

arthropod borne diseases.

VECTORS

Insects that transmit infections are called vectors. Vector-borne transmission can be of two types either mechanical (external) or biological (internal).

1. Mechanical vector: The disease agent is transmitted mechanically by the arthropod.

Examples: Transmission of diarrhea, dysentery, typhoid, food poisoning and

tracghoma by the housely.

2. Biological vectors: Biological vectors are those in whom the pathogens

multiply suciently or has undergone a developmental cycle. The interval

between the time of entry of the pathogen into the vector and the vector

becoming infective is called the extrinsic incubation period.

Examples: Aedes aegypti mosquito in yellow fever, Anopheles mosquito in malaria.

Reservoir hosts: Besides acting as vectors, some insects may also act as

reservoir hosts (for example, ticks in relapsing fever and spotted fever).

Infection is maintained in such insects by transovarial or transstadial passage.

D. SOIL AND WATER

I. SOIL

Some pathogens can survive in the soil for long periods.

Examples

1. Spores of tetanus and gas gangrene: Spores of tetanus and gas gangrene remain viable in the soil for several decades and serve as source of infection.

2. Fungi and parasites: Fungi (causing mycetoma, sporotrichosis,

histoplasmosis) and parasites such as roundworms and hookworms also

survive in the soil and cause human infection.

II. WATER

Water may act as the source of infection either due to contamination with

pathogenic microorganisms (Shigella, Salmonella, Vibrio cholerae, poliomyelitis

virus, hepatitis virus) or due the presence of aquatic vector (cyclops containing

larvae of guinea worm infection).

E. FOOD

1. Contaminated food may act as source of infection of organisms causing food poisoning, gastroenteritits, diarrhea and dysentery.

Q 19. Classification of infection

= The lodgement and multiplication of a parasite in or on the tissues of a host constitute infection. It does not invariably result in disease.

CLASSIFICATION OF INFECTIONS

Infections may be classied in various ways:

1. Primary infection: Initial infection with a parasite in a host is termed primary

infection.

2. Reinfections: Subsequent infections by the same parasite in the host are termed reinfections.

3. Secondary infection: When a new parasite sets up an infection in a host

whose resistance is lowered by a preexisting infectious disease, this is

termed secondary infection.

4. Local infection: The term local infection (more appropriately local sepsis)

indicates a condition where, due to infection or sepsis at localized sites such as appendix or tonsils, generalized effects are produced.

5. Cross-infection: When in a patient already suffering from a disease, a new infection is set up from another host or another external source, it is termed cross-infection.

6. Nosocomial infections: Cross-infections occurring in hospitals are called nosocomial infections (from Greek nosocomion hospital).

7. Iatrogenic infection: The term iatrogenic infection refers to physician induced infections resulting from investigative, therapeutic or other procedures.

8. In apparent infection: In apparent infection is one where clinical effects are not apparent.

9. Subclinical infection: The term subclinical infection is often used as a

synonym to in apparent infection.

10. Atypical infection: Atypical infection is one in which the typical or

characteristic clinical manifestations of the particular infectious disease are not present.

11. Acute infection: An infection which lasts for a relatively short time. (few days to few weeks). E.g. Measles.

12. Chronic infection: An infection which lasts for a long time (over months & years). E.g. TB.

13. Autoinfection: An infection that occurs between two sites on the same host.(worms)

14. Mixed infection: An infection caused by two or more organism.(bacterial vaginosis)

15. Masked infection: An infection is known to occur but the infectious agent cannot be demonstrated.

16. Oppurtunistic infection: An infection with organisms which are normally harmless but become pathogenic when the body's defence mechanisms are compromised.

Q 19. Define carrier & its classification with examples.

= CARRIER

A carrier is person who harbours or lodge of the microorganisms without suffering from any ill effect' because of it. There are several types of carriers:

1. Convalescent carrier: An individual who has recovered from the infectious disease but continues to harbour or lodge large numbers of pathogen.

2. Healthy carrier: A healthy carrier is an individual who harbours or lodge the pathogen but is not ill.

3. Incubatory carrier: An incubatory carrier is an individual who is incubating the pathogen in large numbers but is not yet ill.

4. Temporary carriers: Convalescent, healthy, and incubatory carriers may harbour or lodge the pathogen for only a brief period (hours, days, or weeks) and lasts less than six months.

5. Chronic carriers: They harbour the pathogen for long periods (months, years, or life).

6. Contact carriers: The term contact carrier is applied to a person who acquires the pathogen from a patient.

7. Paradoxical carrier: This refers to a carrier who acquires the pathogens from another carrier.

CHAPTER FOUR

PATHOGENIC ORGANISMS

Q 1.Pathogenicity of staphylococcus aureus.

= Pathogenesis Staph. aureus is an important pyogenic organism and lesions are localised in nature in contrast to streptococcal lesions which are spreading in nature

Thick creamy pus is formed in staphylococcal infections Staphylococcal diseases may be classified as :

cutaneous and deep infections; food poisoning, nosocomial infections, skin exfoliative diseases and toxic shock syndrome.

1. Cutaneous Infections : Superficial infections includes pustules, boils, carbuncles, abscesses, styes, impetigo, pemphigus neonatorum, wound and burn infections.

2. Deep Infections : These include osteomyelitis, tonsillitis, pharyngitis, sinusitis, pneumonitis, empyema, endocarditis, meningitis, bacteriaemia septicaemia and pyaemia.

3. Food Poisoning : Staphylococcal food poisoning may follow 2-6 hours after the ingestion of contaminated food which contains preformed enterotoxin of Stap. aureus.

4. Nosocomial Infections : They are important cause of hospital acquired infections.

5. Skin Exfoliative Diseases : These diseases are produced by the strains of Staph. qureus that produce exfoliative toxin. Stripping of the superficial layers of the skin from the underlying tissue occurs in the various exfoliative syndromes caused by staphylococci (bullous impetigo, pemphigus neonatorum, Ritter's disease). Staphylococcal scalded skin syndrome (SSSS) is one example of exfoliative discases in which toxin spreads systemically.

6. Toxic Shock Syndrome (TSS) :It is caused by toxin shock syndrome toxin (TSST-1). Although TSS became widely known in association with the use of tampons by menstrating women, it occurs in other situations also.

Q 2. Pathogenicity of Streptococcus pyogenes..

= Pathogenesis

Str. pyogenes produces pyogenic infections with a tendency to spread locally. Non-suppurative sequelae of, local infections include acute glomerulonephritis arki rheumatic fever

1. Pyogenic Infections

(i) Respiratory infections

Sore throat (acute tonsillitis and/ or pharyngitis) is the most common of streptococcal diseases. Scariet fever It consists of a combination of sore throat and generalised erythematous rash. It is caused by a strain producing the erythrogenic toxin.

(ii) Skin infections

Str. pyogenes causes suppurative infections of the skin with a predilection to produce lymphangitis and cellulitis. The two typical streptococcal skin infections are erysipelas and impetigo. These skin infections are the main cause leading to acute glomerulonephritis children in the tropics.

(iii) Other pyogenic infections

(a) Puerperal sepsis : Str pyogenes was an important cause of puerperal sepsis, It used to take a heavy toll of life before antibiotres became available.

(b) Sepsis : Infections of skin lesions (eczema, psoriasis, scabies), wounds and burns.

(c) Pyaemia, septicaemia, abscess in internal organs (brain, lung, liver and kidney).

2. **Non-Suppurative Complications**

Str. pyogenes infections are sometimes followed by two important non-suppurative sequelae, acute rheumatic fever and acute glomerulonephritis. These complications occur one to four weeks after the acute infection. Str. pyogenes is no longer detectable when these complications set in. The latent period suggests an immune response. Rheumatic fever is often preceded by sore throat while acute glomerulonephritis by the skin infection. These sequelae or complications are believed to be the result of hypersensitivity to some streptococcal components. Rheunatic fever may follow infection with any serotype of Str. pyogenes while acute glomerulonephritis is caused by only few nephritoginic type.

Q 3.Difference between exotoxins & endotoxins.

= **Exotoxins**

1. They are Lipopolysaccharide in nature.
2. The are heat labile (> 60C)
3. They are actively secreted by living cells into medium.
4. Highly antigenic; stimulates formation of antitoxin that neutralizes.
5. They are converted into toxoid by formaldehyde.
6. Enzymic in action.
7. They have specific pharmacological effect to each toxin.
8. They have very high potency.
9. They are highly specific for particular tissue e.g. tetanus toxin for central nervous system.
10. They do not produce fever in host.
11. They are mainly produced by Gram positive bacteria and also by

some Gram-negative bacteria.

Endotoxins

1. They are protein (polypeptide) and molecular weight 10,000 to

900,00 .

2. Heat stable

3. Form integral part of the cell wall and released on disruption of bacterial cell.

4. Weakly antigenic ; antitoxin is not formed but antibodies against polysaccharides are raised .

5. They can not be toxoided.

6. No enzymic in action.

7. Non specific action of all endotoxins.

8. They have low potency

9.They are non specific in action

10. They produce fever in host

11. They are produced by Gram-negative bacteria.

Q 4 . Pathogenecity of pneumococcus pneumonia.

= Pneumococci colonize the human nasopharynx and may cause infection of the middle ear, paranasal sinuses and respiratory tract by direct spread.

1. Pneumonia

Pneumococci are one of the most common bacteria causing pneumonia, both lobar and bronchopneumonia.

They also cause acute tracheobronchitis and empyema.

Bacteremia may complicate pneumococcal pneumonia.

This can result in metastatic involvement of the meninges, joints and, rarely, the endocardium.

i. Lobar Pneumonia

In adults, types 1-8 are responsible for about 75 percent of cases of pneumococcal pneumonia. In children, types 6, 14, 19 and 23 are frequent causes.

Pneumonia results from aspiration of pneumococci contained in upper airway secretions into the lower respiratory tract. When the normal defences are compromised by viral infection, anesthesia, chilling or other factors, pneumococci multiply, penetrate the bronchial mucosa and spread through the lung along peribronchial tissues and lymphatics. Contiguous spread commonly results in inflammatory involvement of the pleura.

This may progress to empyema. Pericarditis is another uncommon but well recognized complication.

ii. Bronchopneumonia

Bronchopneumonia is almost always a secondary infection. This may be caused by any serotype of pneumococcus. Other causative agents responsible for bronchopneumonia include Staph. aureus, K. pneumoniae, Str. pyogenes, H. influenzae, Fusobacterium species and Bacteroides. Bronchopneumonia is frequently a terminal event in aged and debilitated patients

Q 5 Difference between primary & secondary tuberculosis.

=

Characteristics	*Primary*	*Postprimary*
Site	Any part of lung	Apical region
Local lesion	Small	Large
Cavity formation	Rare	Frequent
Lymphatic involvement	Yes	Minimal
Infectivity[a]	Uncommon	Usual
Tuberculin reactivity	Negative (initially	Positive
Local spread	Uncommon	Frequent

Difference between primary & secondary tuberculosis.

Q 7.Lab. diagnosis for mycobacterium tuberculosis.

= Laboratory Diagnosis

Bacteriological diagnosis can be established by microscopy, culture examination or by animal inoculation test. established by

1. **Specimen**

Specimen collection depends on the site of involvement. Tuberculosis may involve lungs (pulmonary) or sites other than lungs (extrapulmonary).

i) **Pulmonary tuberculosis :** Sputum is the most common specimen. It is collected in a clean wide-mouthed container. A morning specimen may be collected on three consecutive days. If sputum is scanty, a 24 hour specimen may be collected. When sputum is not available, laryngeal swab or bronchial washings are collected. In children, gastric washings may be examined as they tend to swallow sputum.

(ii) Meningitis : Cerebrospinal fluid (CSF) from tuberculous meningus (TBM) often forms a spider web clot on standirg examination of which may be more useful than of fluid.

(iii) Renal tuberculosis : Three consecutive days morning samples of urine are examined.

(iv) Bone and joints tuberculosis :

Aspírated fluid

V) Tissue :

Blopsy of tissue.

1. **Direct Microscopy :**

Smear is made from the specimen and stained by the Ziehl-Neelsen technique It is examined under oil immersion lens. The acid-fast bacilli (AFB) bright red bacilli against a blue background. appear as A negative report should not be given till at least 300 fields have been examined. Grading of smears is done according to number of bacilli seen .If a large number smears are to be examined, fuorescent microscopy is more convenient., Smears are stained with fluorescent dyes such as auramine 'O' or auramine rhodamine and examined under ultraviolet light. The bacilli appear as bright bacilli against dark background.

3. Concentration of Specimens Concentration of a specimen is done to achieve:

(a) homogenisation of the specimen

(b) decontamination i.e. to kill other bacteria present in the specimen.

(c) concentration i.e. to concentrate the bacilli in a small volume without inactivation.

Such concentrate is used for culture and animal inoculation tests besides smear preparation. Several concentration methods are in use.

5. Serology Serology includes detection of anti mycobacterial antibodies in patient serum. Various methods such as enzyme linked immunosorbent assay (ELISA), radio immunoassay (RIA), latex agglutination assay have been employed. Diagnostic utility of these antibodies is equivocal. WHO has banned the use of these tests for diagnosis of active tuberculosis.

6. Molecular Methods Polymerase chain reaction (PCR) is a rapid method in diagnosis of tuberculosis. It is based on DNA amplification and has been used to detect M. tuberculosis directly in clinical specimens.

Q 8 . Pathogenesis of Tuberculosis .

= Pathogenesis**of Tuberculosis:**

The source of infection is usually an open case of pulmonary tuberculosis. The mode of infection is by direct inhalation of aerosolized bacilli contained in droplet nuclei of expectorated sputum tubercle bacilli are acquired from persons with active disease who are excreting viable bacilli by means of coughing, sneezing or talking. Airborne droplet nuclei containing bacteria, 1 to 5 µm, enter the respiratory tract of an exposed individual and are deposited in the lung alveoli. Infection also occurs infrequently by ingestion, for example, through infected milk and rarely by inoculation.

The initial infection with M. tuberculosis is referred to as a primary infection. Subsequent disease in a previously sensitized person, either from an exogenous source or by reactivation of a primary infection, is known as postprimary (secondary or reinfection) tuberculosis with quite different pathological features.

Q9 . Difference between lepromatous & tuberculoid leprosy.

=

Characteristics of lepromatous and tuberculoid leprosy

Feature	Lepromatous leprosy	Tuberculoid (TT) leprosy
1. Resistance	Seen in persons whose resistance is low.	Seen in persons whose resistance is high
2. Skin lesions	Many erythematous macules, papules, or nodules; extensive tissue destruction (e.g., nasal cartilage, bones, ears); diffuse nerve involvement with patchy sensory loss; lack of nerve enlargement.	Few erythematous or hypopigmented plaques with flat centers and raised, demarcated borders; peripheral nerve damage with complete sensory loss; visible enlargement of nerves.
3. Histopathology	Predominantly "foamy" macrophages with few lymphocytes; lack of Langhans' cells; numerous acid-fast bacilli in skin lesions and internal organs.	Infiltration of lymphocytes around center of epithelial cells; presence of Langhans' cells; few or no acid-fast bacilli observed.
4. Infectivity	High	Low
5. Bacilli in skin	+++	-
6. Bacilli in nasal secretions	+++	-
7. Granuloma formation	+++	-
8. Lepromin test	-	+++
9. Antibodies to *M. leprae*	Hypergammaglobulinemia	Normal
10. Erythema nodosum leprosum	Usually present	Erythema nodosum leprosum
11. Prognosis	Poor	Good

Q 10.Pathogenesis of Salmonella Typhi. / enteric fever.

= Pathogenesis

S. typhi, S. paratyphi A and usually S. paratyphi B are confined to human beings. The majority of other salmonellae are primarily infective for animals and human beings are secondarily infected.

Salmonellae cause three types of clinical syndrome in human beings, enteric fever, septicaemia and gastroenteritis.

1 Enteric Fever :

The term enteric fever includes typhoid fever (S. typhi) and paratyphoid fever (S. paraptyphi A, B, C). Infections due to S. typhi and S. paratyphi A are prevalent in India.

i) Typhoid fever : The infection is acquired by ingestion through contaminated food and water. The incubation period is usually 7-14 days. The clinical course may vary from a mild pyrexia to a fatal fulminating disease. The characteristic features are hepatosplenomegaly, step-ladder pyrexia with relative bradycardia and leucopaenia. Skin rashes known as rose-spots may appear during the second or third week.

(ii) Paratyphoid fever : Paratyphoid fever resembles typhoid fever but is milder, S. paratyphi A, B and C cause paratyphoid fever.

Q 11. Laboratory diagnosis of Enteric Fever.

= Laboratory Diagnosis

Bacteriological diagnosis of enteric fever consists of

1. Isolation of bacilli.

2. Demonstration of antibodies.

1. Isolation of Bacilli :

This may be done by culture of specimens like blood, faeces, urine, aspirated duodenal fluid etc. Selection of relevant specimen depends upon duration of illness which is very important for the laboratory diagnosis of enteric fever

2. Demonstration of Antibodies.

Widal Test.

it is an agglutination test for detection of agglutinins (H and 0) in patients with enteric fever. Salmonella antibodles start appearing in the serum at the end of first week and rise sharply during the third week of enteric fever. Two specimens of sera at an interval of 7 to 10 days are preferred to demonstrate a rising antibody titre.

Q 10 . Shigella dysentriae.

= Shigellae cause bacillary dysentery. Humans are the only known reservoir of Shigella organisms infection occurs by ingestion. The infection is highly communicable because of the low infective dose required to produce the disease. The minimum infective dose is low, as few as 10-100 bacilli being capable of initiating the disease, probably because they survive gastric acidity

better than other enterobacteria. Shigella spp. are pathogens of man and other primates, and the pathogenesis

of infection with these bacteria and entero-invasive E.

coli (EIEC) is very similar.

Shigella cause disease by invading and replicating in cells lining the colonic mucosa. After reaching the largeb intestine, the shigellae multiply in the gut lumen. The shigellae multiply within the epithelial cells and spread laterally into adjacent cells, where cell-to-cell passage

occurs, and deep into the lamina propria. The infected

epithelial cells are killed and the lamina propria and

submucosa develop an inflammatory reaction with capillary thrombosis.

Bacillary dysentery has a short incubation period

(1-7 days, usually 48 hours). The onset and clinical

course are variable and are largely determined by the

virulence of the infecting strain. The clinical manifestations of shigellosis vary from asymptomatic to severe

forms of the disease. The main clinical features are frequent passage of loose, scanty feces containing blood

and mucus, along with abdominal cramps and tenesmus. Fever and vomiting may be present. Infection is

usually self-limited, although antibiotic treatment is

recommended to reduce the risk of secondary spread to

family members and other contacts.

In dysentery caused by S. dysenteria type 1, patients

experience more severe symptoms.

Q 11. Pathogenesis of E.coli.

= Pathogenesis Esch. coli forms a part of normal intestinal flora of man and animal. There are four major types of clinical syndromes which are caused by Esch. coli:

(1) urinary, tract infection

(2) diarrhoea

(3) pyogenic infections, and

(4) septicaemia.

1. Urinary Tract

Infection Esch. coli is the commonest organism responsible for urinary tract infection (UTI). Esch, coli that cause UTI often originates in the intestine of the patient.

2. Diarrhoea Esch. coli causing diarrhoeal diseases are of four groups. They produce diarrhoea with different pathogenic mechanisms.

(i) Enteropathogenic Esch, coli (EPEC)

EPEC adhere tightly to enterocytes, leading inflammatory reactions and epithelial degenerae changes.

i i) Enterotoxigemic Esch. coli (ETEC) These are the strains that form a heat- labile enterotoxin (LT) or a heat-stable enterotoxin (ST) or both. They are now known to be a major cause of diarrhoea in children in developing countries and are the most important cause of travellers diarrhoea. The name travellers' diarrhoea refers to diarrhoea in persons from the developed countries within a few days of their visit to one of the developing countries.

(iii) Enteroinvasive Esch. coli (EIEC) Some strains of Esch. coli invade the intestinal epithelial cells as do dysentery bacilli and produce disease identical to shigella dysentery. These have been named enteroinvasive Esch. coli (EIEC). On instillation into the eyes of guinea pigs, EIEC cause keratoconjunctivitis, this diagnostic test for EIEC is called Sereny test.

(iv) Enterohaemorrhagic Esch coli (EHEC) or Verocytotorin producing Esch, coli (VTEC) haemorrhagic These strains cause and haemolytic uraemic syndrome (HUS). Toxin responsible is called Verotoxin' because of its effect vero cells in culture.

3. Pyogenic Infections Esch. coli may cause wound infection, peritonitis, cholecystitis and neonatal meningitis. It is an important cause of neonatal meningitis.

4. Septicaemia Esch. coli is a very common cause of septicaerria in many hospitals. This condition usually occurs in debilitated patients and mnortality is very high.

Q 12. Difference between Amoebic & Bacillary dysentery.

=

FEATURES	AMOEBIC DYSENTERY	BACILLARY DYSENTERY
Causative agent	Entomoeba histolytica	Shigella species, Enterohemorrhagic E. coli, Vibrio para-hemolyticus, Campylobacter jejuni
Nature of lesion	Necrotic due to proteolytic ferment	Suppurative due to diffusible toxins
Depth of ulcer	Usually deep	Shallow
Margin of ulcer	Ragged and undermined	Uniform, clear-cut (sharp)
Intervening mucos	Normal	Inflamed
Type of necrosis (cellular level)	Pyknotic (pyknotic body and mouse eaten cells)	Karyolysis (ghost cell and ring nucleus)
Liver abscess	Common	Rare
Cellular response	Mononuclear	Polymorphonuclear

symptoms	Amoebic dysentery	Bacillary dysentery
Occurrence	Usu. In the form of sporadic cases	Usu. In the form of outbreaks
Onset	gradual	Acute
Fever	Usu. Low grade (may be high in case of liver abscess)	High grade
Tenesmus/Abd. Cramps	Moderate	Very severe
Stool	Foul- smelling	Not foul-smelling
RBCs	In clumps	Discrete
Pus cells	Scanty	Numerous
Eosinophils	Present	Absent or rare
Bacteria	Numerous, motile	Scanty, non-motile
E. histolytica	Trophozoites +	Absent
Growth on culture	Negative	Positive

Q 13 . Pathogenesis of diarrhoea.

= Diarrhoea Esch. coli causing diarrhoeal diseases are of four groups. They produce diarrhoea with different pathogenic mechanisms.

(i) Enteropathogenic Esch, coli (EPEC)

EPEC adhere tightly to enterocytes, leading inflammatory reactions and epithelial degenerae changes.

ii) Enterotoxigemic Esch. coli (ETEC) These are the strains that form a heat- labile enterotoxin (LT) or a heat-stable enterotoxin (ST) or both. They are now known to be a major cause of diarrhoea in children in developing countries and are the most important cause of travellers diarrhoea. The name travellers' diarrhoea refers to diarrhoea in persons from the developed countries within a few days of their visit to one of the developing countries.

(iii) Enteroinvasive Esch. coli (EIEC) Some strains of Esch. coli invade the intestinal epithelial cells as do dysentery bacilli and produce disease identical to shigella dysentery. These have been named enteroinvasive Esch. coli (EIEC). On instillation into the eyes of guinea pigs, EIEC cause keratoconjunctivitis, this diagnostic test for EIEC is called Sereny test.

(iv) Enterohaemorrhagic Esch coli (EHEC) or Verocytotorin producing Esch, coli (VTEC) haemorrhagic These strains cause and haemolytic uraemic syndrome (HUS). Toxin responsible is called Verotoxin' because of its effect vero cells in culture.

Q 14. Enlist organisms causing diarrhea

=

Table. 78.9: Causative agents of infective diarrhea

A. Bacteria
- *Vibrio cholerae*
- *V. parahaemolyticus*
- ***Escherichia coli*** (ETEC, EPEC)
- ***Salmonella Enteritidis***
- S. Typhimurium
- Other Salmonella sp.
- ***Campylobacter*** sp.
- ***Yersinia enterocolitica***
- ***Shigella*** sp.
- *Clostridium perfringens*
- *C. difficile*
- ***Staphylococcus aureus***
- ***Bacillus cereus***
- *Aeromonas hydrophilia*
- *Plesiomonas shigelloides*

B. Viruses
- Rotavirus
- Astrovirus
- Calicivirus
- Norwalk virus
- Adenovirus

C. Protozoa
- *Entamoeba histolytica*
- *Giardia lamblia*
- *Cryptosporidium parvum*
- *Isospora belli*

D. Cestodes
- ***Hymenolepis nana***

E. Nematodes
- *Trichuris trichiura*
- *Strongyloides stercoralis*
- *Ascaris lumbricoides*
- *Hookworms*

F. Trematodes
Schistosoma mansoni

Organisms causing diarrhea

Q 15. Write a short note on laboratory diagnosis of diarrhea.

= Laboratory Diagnosis

1. Collection of Specimens

In most cases the stool is sent for bacterial culture. Because there are many other potential pathogens, the laboratory must be informed which tests to perform.

2. Direct Microscopy

Microscopic examination of the stool may reveal white blood cells if the patient has an inflammatory diarrhea. The bacterial pathogen may be visible on direct microscopic examination of the stool. In general, a wet film of a concentrate of the feces should be examined for protozoa, protozoal cysts and helminthes ova, and a stained film for the oocysts of cryptosporidium.

3. Culture

Selective and differential culture media are commonly used to attempt to identify bacterial pathogens in stool. The differential aspect of the media often allows differentiation of bacterial species based on colony morphology; the differences in colony appearance are usually due to different biochemical characteristics of the organisms.

a. Vibrios

Culture: Selective media such as TCBS or bile salt agar are used. Culture plates are incubated at 37°C for 24-48 hours. Vibrio parahaemolyticus is a halophilic vibrio in media containing sodium chloride.

Identification: Identification of isolates is done by colony morphology, biochemical reactions and slide agglutination test.

b. Esch. coli

(i) ETEC; (ii) EPEC; (iii) EIEC; (iv) EAEC

i. Culture: Cuture is done on blood agar and MacConkey's agar. These media are incubated at 37°C for 24 hours.

ii. Identification: Identification of isolates is done by colony morphology, biochemical reactions, slide agglutination with antisera. For the identification of EIEC strains Sereny test is used. Another method for identification of these strains is invasion of cultured HeLa cells. Production of verocytotoxin (VT) is confirmed by testing the strains on Vero cells, in which they cause cytopathic effects.

Q 15. Blood Culture.

= Blood Culture

A blood culture is a medical laboratory test used to detect bacteria or fungi in a person's blood. Blood is normally sterile, and the presence of microbes in the blood often indicates a serious bloodstream infection such as a bacteremia, or fungemia, that can result in sepsis.

The test involves drawing the blood into bottles containing chemicals that encourage microbial growth, which are then placed in an incubator for several days to allow the organisms to multiply. If microbial growth is detected, a Gram stain is made from the blood culture bottle to confirm that bacteria are present and to provide a preliminary identification. The blood is then inoculated onto an agar plate to isolate the organisms for further testing.A positive Gram stain from a blood culture is considered a critical result and must immediately be reported to the clinician.

To ensure accurate results, blood cultures are drawn using sterile technique. If the sample is contaminated with skin flora, the person will appear to have those organisms in their blood. When a blood culture is performed, it is usually drawn in at least two different sets (one set of bottles from each arm) so that contamination is easier to detect. If an organism only appears in one of the two sets, it is more likely to be a contaminant.

When a patient shows signs or symptoms of a systemic infection, results from a blood culture can verify that an infection is present, and they can identify the type (or types) of microorganism that is responsible for the infection. For example, blood tests can identify the causative organisms in severe pneumonia, puerperal fever, pelvic inflammatory disease, neonatal epiglottitis, sepsis, and fever of unknown origin (FUO). However, negative growths do not exclude infection.

Q 16. Blood smear

= A blood sample is used to look for abnormalities in the number and shape of blood cells, presence of parasites.

A blood smear, also referred to as a peripheral smear for morphology, is an important test for evaluating blood-related problems, such as those in red blood cells, white blood cells, or platelets. It has a wide range of uses, including distinguishing viral infections from bacterial infections, evaluating anemia, looking for causes of jaundice, and even diagnosing malaria.

Unlike automated tests (such as a CBC), a technician or physician looks at a blood smear under the microscope in order to detect a wide range of changes that give clues to underlying diseases.

Purpose of Test

A blood smear involves looking at a sample of blood under the microscope after applying special stains and looking for abnormalities or changes in red blood cells, white blood cells, and platelets.

There are many reasons why your doctor may order a blood smear. Some of these include:

- to further evaluate abnormalities found on a complete blood count (CBC) such as a high or low red blood cell count, white blood cell count, or platelet count.
- to evaluate an infection (identifying the types of white blood cells present can help determine if an infection is viral, bacterial, or parasitic, as well as the severity)
- to look for causes of unexplained jaundice
- as part of a work-up for people who have unexplained weight loss (defined as a loss of 5 percent of body weight over a 6 month period without trying)
- to evaluate symptoms of lightheadedness and palor (paleness)

- to look for causes of petechiae, bruising, or excess bleeding
- with a low platelet count, to determine if the cause is increased degradation or decreased production (based on the size)
- to investigate findings suspicious for blood-related cancers
- to look for malaria
- to confirm sickle cell disease
- to evaluate symptoms of bone pain
- to look for causes of enlargement of the spleen, liver, or lymph nodes.

A blood smear looks for the numbers and characteristics of the three types of blood cells:

- **Red blood cells** (RBCs) are the cells that transport oxygen to the tissues
- **White blood cells** (WBCs) are cells that fight infection among several other functions
- **Platelets** are cell fragments that play an important role in blood clotting.

Q 17. Enumerate the organism causing urinary track infection.

= E. coli and coliforms account for the large majority of naturally acquired urinary tract infections. Those acquired in the hospital, following instrumentation, are more often caused by other bacteria such as Pseudomonas and Proteus. Most frequently encountered O serotypes of E. coli in UTI include O1, O2, O4, O6, O7, O18 and O75. These arealso known as nephritogenic strains.

E. coli that cause UTI often originate in the gut of the patient. The bacteria may gain access to the urinary tract by the ascending or the hematogenous route.

1. Other members of family Enterobacteriaceae that usually cause UTI are Kiebsiella, Proteus, Citrobacter, and those which

rarely produce UTI are salmonellae, edwardsiellae and Enterobacter.

2. The gram-positive organisms which can cause UTI are Staphylococcus aureus, coagulase-negative staphylococci, Streptococcus faecalis, S. pyogenes, S. agalactiae, S. milleri, other streptococci and anaerobic streptococci.

3. Rarely, Gardnerella vaginalis may cause UTI.

4. Candida albicans may cause UTI in diabetic and immunocompromised patients.

5. The hospital-associated infection following instrumentation and catheterization is mostly caused by Pseudomonas and Proteus.

Q 18. Write down the laboratory diagnosis of Urinary track infection (UTI).

= Laboratory Diagnosis

URINARY TRACT INFECTION

Normal urine is sterile, but during voiding may become contaminated with commensals of genital

1. Specimen Collection Midstream urine specimen (MSU)

collected preferably prior to administration of antibiotics. Specimen is collected in a sterile container. (Before collecting a sample, genitalia should be cleaned with soap and water and men are instructed to retract the foreskin of glans penis whereas women should keep the labia apart.(The first portion of urine is allowed to pass, then without interrupting the urine low, mid-portion of the stream is collected. The first portion of urine adequately lushes out the normal urethral flora.)

ii) Catheter specimen

Urine should be collected directly from the catheter and not from the collection bag ,The catheter should hot touch the container. Although a catheter specimen yields excellent results but catheterisation to obtain urine is not justified because of risk of introducing infection.

(iii) Urine specimens from infants

A clean catch specimen after cleansing of genitalia is preferred. 2. Transport As urine is a good culture medium, specimens after collection should reach the laboratory with minimum delay, if it is not possible, the specimen is to be refrigerated at 4°C.

3. Laboratory Methods Part of the specimen is used for bacteriological culture and the rest is examined immediately under the microscope.

(i) Microscopy Urine is centrifuged and deposit is examined under the microscope for detecting pus cells, erythrocytes, epithelial cells and bacteria.

(ii) Culture Most laboratories use a semiquantitative method (standard loop technique) for culture of urine specimens.

(iii) Identification The organisms are identified by colony characters Grams staining, motility, biochemical reactions and slide agglutination test."

Antibiotic sensitivity test Esch. coli and other common urinary pathogens develop multiple drug resistance. Antibiotic sensitivity is necessary to administer proper antibiotics.

Q19. Widal Test .

= Widal test: In the Widal test used for the diagnosis of enteric fever, two types of antigens are used: the flagellar antigens (H) and somatic (O) antigen.

H antigen is a formolised suspension of the organisms which combining with its antibody, forms large, loose and fluffy clumps resembling wisps of cotton-wool. Conical Dreyer's tubes are used for H agglutination. O (somatic) antigen is prepared by treating the bacterial suspension with alcohol.

It forms tight, compact deposits resembling chalk powder at the base of round-bottomed (Felix) tubes on combination with antibody. Agglutinated bacilli spread out in a disk like pattern at the bottom of thetube, whereas, negative reaction shows a compact button likedeposit.

Q 20. Describe the normal microbial flora of different body parts.

= Normal Flora refers to the population of microorganisms that inhabit skin and mucous membranes of normal human body.

A healthy foetus in-utero is free from micoorganisms. During birth the infant is exposed to vaginal flora. Within a few hours of birth, oral and nasopharyngeal flora develops and in a day or two resident flora of the lower intestine appears. The normal microbial flora is more or less constant for each species of animal.

1 NORMAL FLORA OF THE SKIN

The skin contains 10^2 to 10^1 organisms per cm^2. Bathing has little effect on the resident flora of the skin. Staph epidermidis and diphtheroids are numerous and most constant in the skin. Other microorganisms include Peptococcus, Str viridans, Enterococcus, Micrococcus, Esch. coli, Proteus, Candida albicans, and Propionibacterium aono. Penicillin resistant staphylococci are seen individuals working in hospitals.

II. NORMAL FLORA OF THE CONJUNCTIVA

The conjunctiva is relatively free from bacteria due to the flushing action of tears and due to the presence of lysozyme in it. The predominant organisms are Coryne- bacterium xerosis, Staph. epidermidis, Moraxella species and non-haemolytic streptococci.

iii. NORMAL FLORA OF THE NOSE AND NASOPHARYNX

The flora of nose harbours diphtheroids, staphylococci, streptococci and Haemophilus species. The nasopharynx of the infant is sterile at birth but, within 2-3 days after birth, acquires the flora carried by tne mother and the attendants. The nasopharynx is a natural habitat of the common pathogens which cause infections of the nose, throat, bronchi and lungs.

IV. NORMAL FLORA OF THE MOUTH

The mouth contains micrococci, Gram positive aerobic spore bearing bacilli, coliforms, Proteus and lactobacilli. The gum pockets between the teeth have a wide spectrum anaerobic bacilli, anaerobic micrococci, microaerophilic and anaerobic streptococci, vibrios, fusiform bacilli. Corynebacterium species, actinomyces, mycoplasma and bacteroides are all found in varying extent. The mouth of infant is not sterile at birth. It generally contains the same organisms as those present in mother's vagina i.e. a mixture of micrococci, streptococci, coliform bacilli and Doderlien's bacilli. These organisms diminish in number during the first 2-5 days after birth and are replaced by the bacteria present in the mouth of the mother.

V. NORMAL FLORA OF THE UPPER RESPIRATORY TRACT

Within 12 hours after birth alpha haemolytic streptococci are present in the upper respiratory tract. They become the dominant organism of the oropharynx and remain so for life. In the pharynx and trachea, flora is similar to that of the mouth. A few bacteria are present in normal bronchi, but smaller bronchi and alveoli are normally sterile.

VI. NORMAL FLORA OF THE GASTROINTESTINAL TRACT

The gastrointestinal tract of the foetus in-utero is sterile. It becomes contaminated with organisms shortly after birth. In breast fed infants, the intestine contains lactobacilli, enterococci, colon bacilli and staphylococci. In bottle fed infants, the intestine contains Leptotrichia, anaerobic lactobacilli, colon bacilli and aerobic and anaerobic spore-bearing organisms. Due to low pH of the stomach, it is virtually sterile except soon after eating, As the acidic pH of

the stomach becomes alkaline in the intestine, the number of bacteria increases progressively beyond the duodemum to the colon. The bacterial count is low in small intestine compared to that in large intestine.

Q 21 . Describe Organisms causing sore throat .

= Sore throat is essentially an acute tonsillitis or

pharyngitis. It is characterized by redness and edema of mucosa, exudation of tonsils, pseudomembrane formation, edema of uvula, gray coating of tongue and enlargement of cervical lymph nodes.

Causative agents of sore throat are given in Table :

Table: Causative agents of sore throat

A. Bacteria

- Streptococcus β-hemolytic group A and occasionally groups C and G
- Corynebacterium diphtheriae
- Haemophilus influenzae
- Bordetella pertussis
- Neisseria gonorrhoeae
- Treponema vincentii
- Leptotrichia buccalis

B. Fungi

- Candida albicans

C. Viruses

- Epstein-Barr virus
- Adenoviruses
- Coxsackievirus A

Q 22. Write a Short Note on Food poising .

= The term bacterial food poisoning is restricted to acute gastroenteritis due to the presence of bacteria, usually in large numbers, or their products in food.

It is of three types

A. Infective type: In this type, multiplication of bacteria occurs in vivo when infective doses of microorganisms are ingested with food. Incubation period is generally 8 to 24 hours.

The typical example of this type of food poisoning is by Salmonellae.

B. Toxic type: In this type, the disease follows ingestion of food with preformed toxin. Incubation period is short (2 to 6 hours). Example is staphylococcal

food poisoning.

Causative agents of food poisoning

1. Infectlve type

- Salmonella typhimurium
- S. Enteritidis
- S. Heidelberg
- S. Indiana
- S. Newport
- S. Dublin
- Vibrio parahaemolyticus
- Campylobacter jejuni

2. Toxic type

- Staphylococcus aureus.

Bacillus cereus

- Clostridm botulinum

3. Infectlve—toxic type

Clostridium perfringens

C. Infective-toxic type: In this type, bacteria release

the toxin in the bowel. The incubation period is 6 to 12 hours. The typical example is C. perfringens food poisoning.

For the laboratory diagnosis, refer to the corresponding chapters. It has also been described earlier under "Laboratory Diagnosis of Diarrhea".

Q 23. Describe life cycle of malarial parasite.

= Malaria is the mosquito born infectious disease of human. Malaria is caused by a parasite that is passed from one human to another by the bite of infected Anopheles mosquitoes. After infection, the parasites (called sporozoites) travel through the bloodstream to the liver, where they mature and release another form, the merozoites. which introduces the protists via its saliva into the circulatory system, and ultimately to the liver where they mature and reproduce.

Intermediate host : human

- Final host : mosquito
- Infective stage : sporozoite
- Infective way : mosquito bite skin of human

- Parasitic position : liver and red blood cells
- Transmitted stage : gametocytes
- Schizogonic cycle in red cells : 48 hrs/P.v
- Sporozoite : tachysporozite and bradysporozite

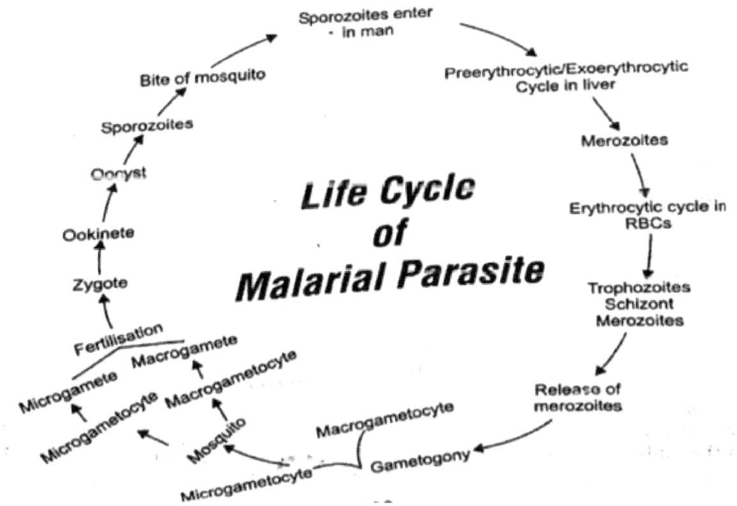

Life cycle of malarial parasite

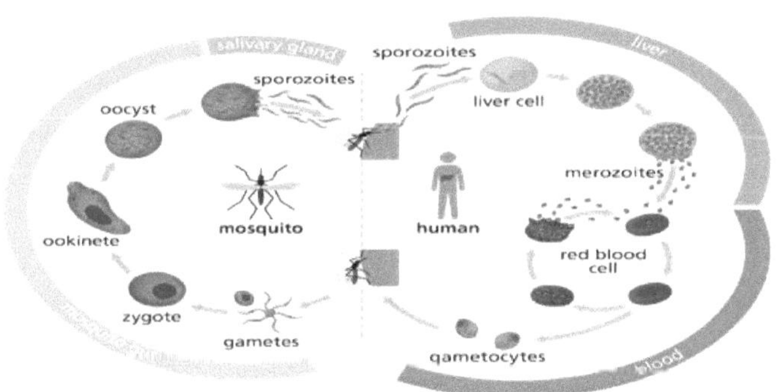

Life cycle of malarial parasite

Q 24. Write a short note on lab diagnosis of malaria.

= Lab Diagnosis

Method used to diagnose:

1. Microscopy Serology
2. Rapid Diagnostic Tests
3. Molecular biology method (PCR)

Microscopy

Gold standard

Highly sensitive, specific

Laboratory diagnosis of malaria can by made through microscopic examination of thick or thin blood smear .

Thick smears are used for screening purposes

Thin smears are for morphological detail and species identification.

The mainstay of malaria diagnosis has been the microscopic examination of blood, utilizing blood films Although blood is the sample most frequently used to make a diagnosis, both saliva and urine have been investigated as alternative, less invasive specimens. More recently, modern techniques utilizing antigen tests or polymerase chain reaction have been discovered, though these are not widely implemented in malaria endemic regions . Areas that cannot afford laboratory diagnostic tests often use only a history of subjective fever as the indication to treat for malaria.

Q 25. Draw well labelled diagram of emberyonated egg.

=

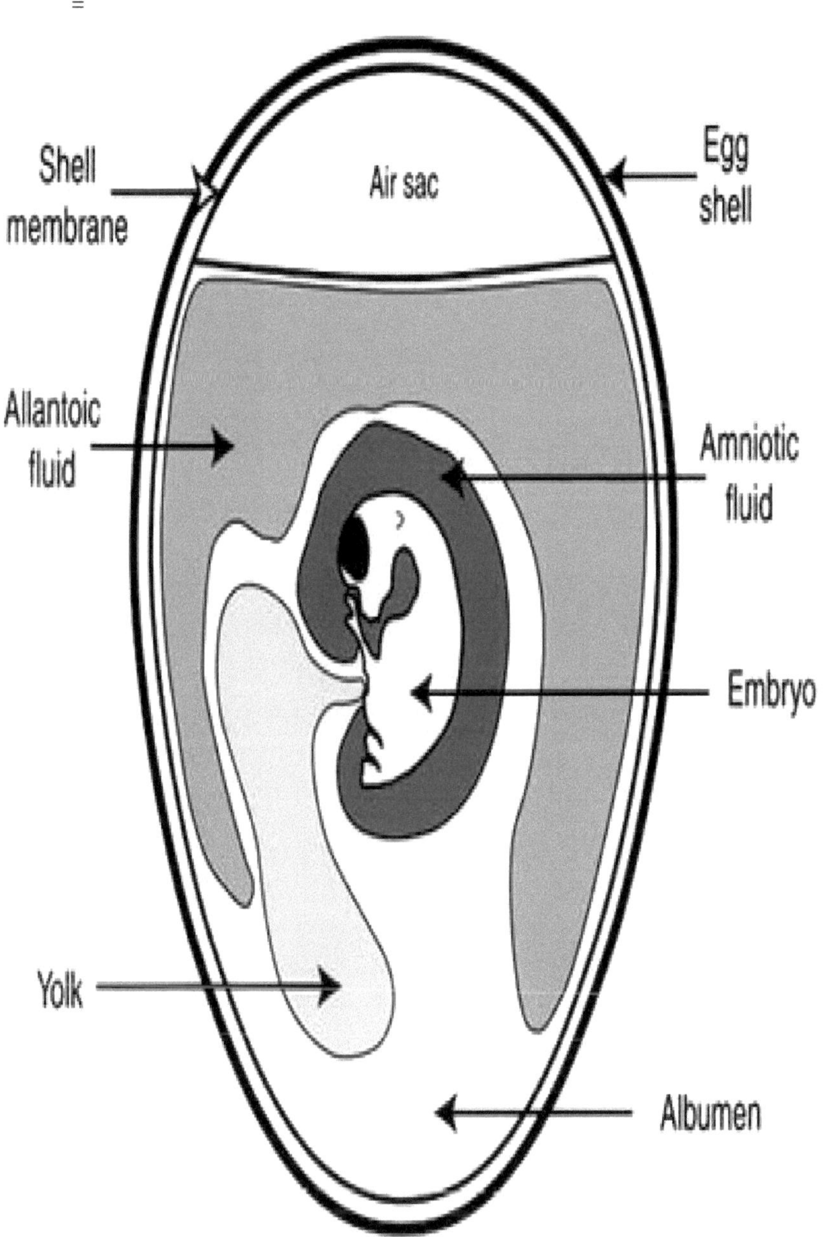

Q 26 . Draw well diagram of HIV viruses .

=

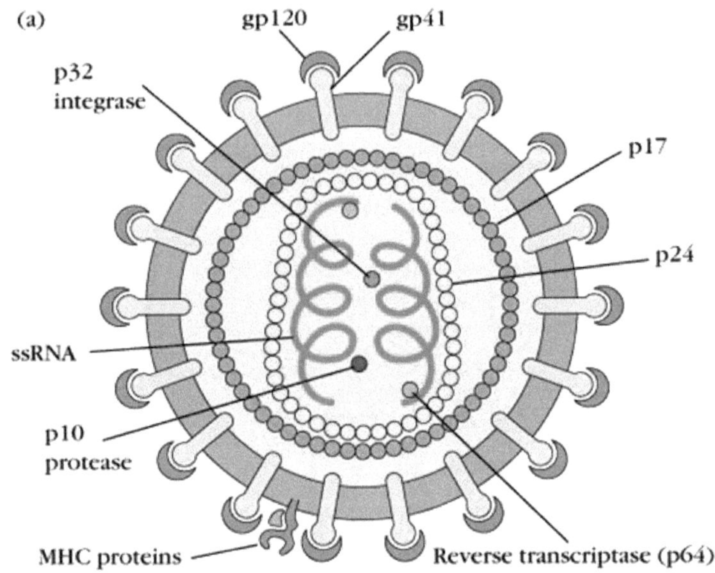

HIV viruses

Q 27. Write down the causes / Routes / Modes of the HIV infection.

= **Routes of Transmission**

Virus is present in the blood, semen, and cervical and vaginal secretions, and these sources are important in transmission. HIV is spread only by three modes:

1. Sexual contact with infected persons (heterosexual or homosexual);

2. By blood and blood products;

3. From infected mother to babies (intrapartum, perinatal, postnatal).

The modes of transmission of HIV and their relative

risks are shown in Tables

1. Sexual Intercourse

HIV is primarily a sexually transmitted infection. Heterosexual transfer of virus is the route by which the great majority of infections are spread, accounting for 90 percent of the global total. Both sexes are affected equally. Transmission in the developing countries is almost always heterosexual and can take place in both directions.

The presence of other sexually transmitted diseases such as syphilis, gonorrhea, or herpes simplex type 2 increases the risk of sexual HIV transmission as much as a hundred-fold.

Sex workers are at high risk due to their large number of partners;

Most early studies established that unprotected anal intercourse was a particular risk, especially to the passive, receptive partner . The risk increases in proportion to the number of sexual encounters with different partners.

Table 68.4: Transmission of HIV Infection

Routes	*Specific Transmission*
Known Routes of Transmission	
1. Inoculation in blood	Transfusion of blood and blood products Needle sharing among intravenous drug abusers Needlestick, open wound, and mucous membrane exposure in health care workers Tattoo needles
2. Sexual transmission	Anal and vaginal intercourse
3. Mother to baby	Intrauterine transmission Peripartum transmission Breast milk

2. Blood and Blood Products

Transfusion of infectious blood or blood products is an effective route for viral transmission.

Contaminated Needles

This is particularly relevant in drug addicts who share syringes and needles. Drug and sexual routes merge when misusers support their habit by prostitution.

The use of unsterile syringes and needles by qualified and unqualified health workers makes iatrogenic.

Contamination of eyes and mucous membranes is

another possible route, but this is seldom confirmed.

Tattoo needles and contaminated inks are other potential means by which HIV can be transmitted.

3. Mother to Child Transmission

Transmission of infection from mother to baby can take

place before, during or after birth. Mother-to-infant

transmission rates vary from 13 to 40 percent in untreated women Infants can become infected in utero, during the birth process, or, more commonly, through breast feeding. Transmission during breast

feeding usually occurs early (by 6 months).

Q 28 Write the stages of the HIV infection

= The natural evolution of HIV infection can be considered in the following stages.

The acute seroconversion illness resembles glandular fever, with adenopathy and flu-like symptoms.Within 3-6 weeks of infection with HIV, about 50 percent of persons experience low grade fever, malaise, headache, lymphadenopathy, sometimes with rash and arthropathy resembling glandular fever.

During this period there is a very high level of virus replication occurring in CD4+ cells.

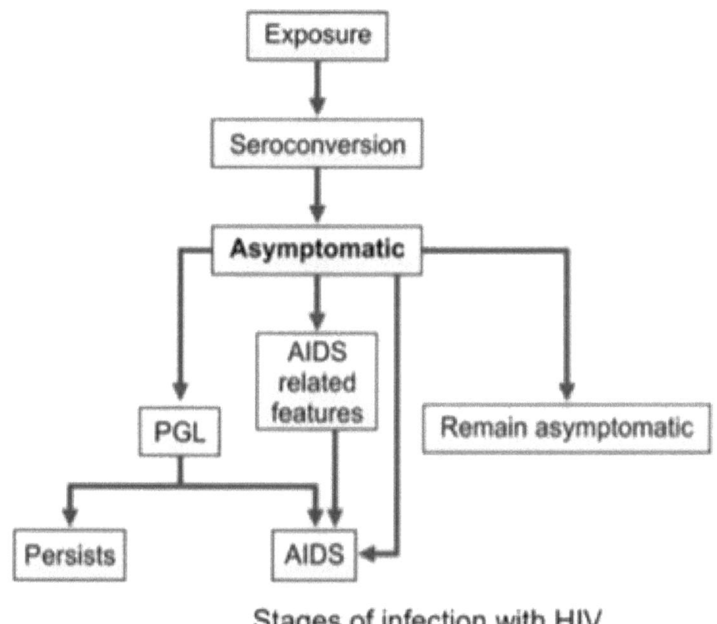

Stages of infection with HIV

stages of the HIV infection

Tests for HIV antibodies are usually negative at the onset of the illness but become positive during its course. Hence this syndrome has been called 'seroconversion' illness.

Asymptomatic or Latent Infection

A clinically asymptomatic or "latent" period follows the acute infection. During this time, there is a high level of ongoing viral replication. They show positive HIV antibody tests during this phase and are infectious. The infection progresses in course of time through various stages, CD4 lymphocytopenia, minor opportunistic infections, persistent generalized lymphadenopathy, AIDS-related complex (ARC), ultimately terminating in full blown AIDS, with its characteristic infections and malignancies.

The time from infection to death may be as long as 10 years and is inevitable in 70 percent of infected persons.

Persistent Generalized Lymphadenopathy (PGL) :

Persistent generalized lymphadenopathy (PGL) is present in 25-30 percent of patients who are otherwise asymptomatic . This has been defined as the presence of enlarged lymph nodes, at least 1 cm in diameter, in two or more noncontiguous extrainguinal sites, that persist for at least three months, in the absence of any current illness or medication that may cause lymphadenopathy. The rate of progression of patients with PGL to AIDS is no greater than in those without adenopathy. This by itself is benign but the cases may progress to ARC or AIDS.

AIDS Related Complex (ARC)

This group includes patients with considerable immunodeficiency, suffering from various constitutional symptoms or minor opportunistic infections. The typical constitutional symptoms are fatigue, unexplained fever, persistent diarrhea and marked weight loss of more than 10 percent of body weight.

ARC patients are usually severely ill and many of them progress to AIDS in a few months. With no treatment, the interval between primary infection with HIV and the first appearance of clinical disease is usually long in adults, averaging about 8-10 years. Death occurs about 2 years later.

AIDS

This is the end-stage disease representing the irreversible breakdown of immune defence mechanisms, leaving the patient prey to progressive opportunistic infections and malignancies. AIDS may be manifested in several different ways, including lymphadenopathy and fever,opportunistic infections, malignancies, and AIDS-related dementia.

Q 29. Pathogenesis of HIV & AIDS .

=

PATHOGENESIS

- HIV virus enters in the blood of foetus through the placenta of infected mother OR through anyother mode of transmission

- Than the virus comes in contact with CD4 lymphocytes

- It binds with CD4 antigen present on the T lymphocytes and B lymphocytes

- After binding the virus enters the cell

- Inside the cell,the virus genome uncoats and with the help of reverse transcriptase, converts the single RNA into double stranded DNA

- This DNA integrates into the infected cell genome

- This integration causes the formation of HIV virus progeny with the help of host cell

Pathogenesis of HIV & AIDS

Q 30 . Write down the laboratory diagnosis of HIV/ Aids.

= Laboratory Diagnosis

1.Specific Tests for HIV Infections

(i) Antigen detection.

The p24 antigen is the earliest virus marker to appear in the blood. ELISA can be used for detection of this antigen. Virus isolation is an important test for diagnosis in window period when antibodies are absent in serum of patient.

(ii) Virus isolation

For diagnosis, virus is not routinely isolated. It can be isolated from CD4 lymphocytes of peripheral blood, bone-marrow and serum. Virus isolation is an Important test for diagnosis in window period when antibodies are absent in serum of patient.

(iii) Detection of viral nucleic acid

Viral nucleic acid can be detected by polymerase chain reaction (PCR). The test is highly sensitive and specific. It is also useful for diagnosis in window period.

(v)Antibody detection

Demonstration of antibodies is the simplest and most commonly employed technique for diagnosis. It may take several weeks to months for antibodies to appear after infection. HIV infected persons remain negative for antibodies during window period, when initial viral replication takes place for about 2-3 weeks. There are two types of serological tests-screening and supplemental.

Screening tests

a. ELISA test:

ELISA is the method most commonly used. It is highly sensitive and specific test. It is an extremely good screening test and most laboratories use a commercial ELISA kit that contains both HIV-1 and HIV-2. Saliva is an acceptable alternative to serum for antibody testing by ELISA.

(b) Rapid tests: These tests take less than 30 minutes and do not require expensive equipment. The rapid tests include dot-blot assay, particle agglutination, HIV spot and comb tests.

c) Simple tests: They take 1-2 hours and do not require expensive equipment.

Supplemental test –

Western blot test:

In this test, HIV proteins are separated and these proteins are blotted on to strips of nitrocellulose paper. These strips are reacted with test sera. Antibodies to HIV proteins, if present in test serum, combine with different fragments of HIV. The position of the colour band on the strip indicates the fragment of antigen with which antibodies have reacted.

Q 31. Life cycle of Ascaris Lumbricoid (Round Worm).

= Life Cycle Ascaris lumbricoides passes its life cycle in only one host, man. No intermediate host is required. Man is the only definitive host. Adult worms live the jejunum of man. Fertilised eggs containing the unsegmented ova are passed in the faeces. These eggs are not immediately infective to man.

Egg undergo development in soil. A rhabditiform larva is developed from unsegmented ovum and undergoes first moulting within the egg shell.

These eggs containing rhabditiform larvae are pathogenic to man. Man acquires infection by ingestion of food, drink of raw vegetables contaminated with eggs containing rhabditiform larvae (embryonated eggs).

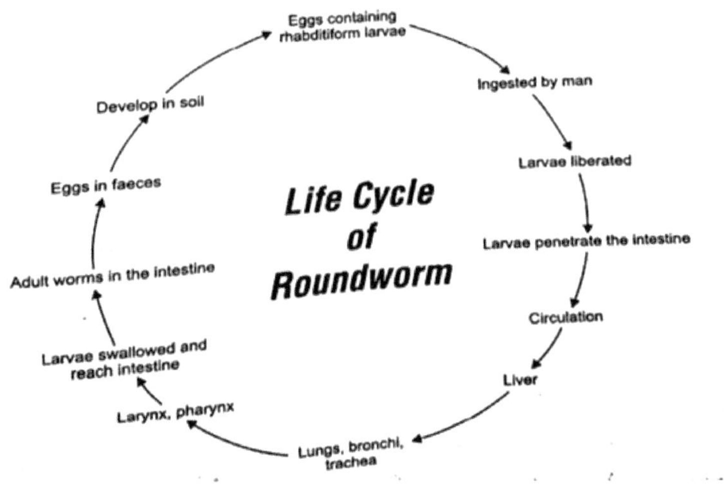

Life cycle of Ascaris Lumbricoid (Round Worm)

In the upper Part of the small intestine (duodenum), rhabditiform larvae are liberated from the embryonated eggs. These newly hatched larvae then burrow their way through the mucous membrane of the small intestine and are

caried by the portal circulation to the liver. They then pass out of the liver and via right heart enter the pulmonary circulation. In the lungs they grow much bigger in size and moult twice. They break through he capillary wall and reach the lung alveoli. From the larvae crawl up the bronchi and trachea and e propelled into the larynx and pharynx and are Srallowed. They pass down the oesophagus to the stomach and localise in the upper part of the small intestine, their normal abode. Another moulting takes place. The larvae grow into adult worms and sexual maturity occurs. The gravid female begins to discharge eggs in the stool and the life cycle is again repeated.

Q 32. List 4 DNAviruses and 4RNA viruses .

= DNA Viruses

Sometimes referred to as the HHAPPPy viruses:

Herpes

Hepadna

? Adeno

? Papova

? Parvo

? Pox

? Most

DNA viruses are double-stranded, show icosahedral symmetry, and replicate in the nucleus.

DNA Viruses

1. Parvoviridae Family :

Three genera have been described: Parvovirus, Adenosatellovirus and Densovirus.

2. Hepadnaviridae Family :

This consists of the human hepatitis type B virus and related viruses of animals and birds. (The name comes from hepa = liver, and dna for DNA core). Three viral types are known that infect mammals (humans, woodchucks, and ground squirrels) and another that infects ducks.

4. Papovaviridae Family :

Two genera have been recognized—Papillomavirus and Polyomavirus.

Papillomavirus are also a former member of the Papovaviridae family. Polyomaviruses were formerly a part of the Papovaviridae family before it was split into two families.

5. Adenoviridae Family :

Members have been classified into two genera: Mastadenovirus (mammalian adenoviruses) and Aviadenovirus (adenoviruses of birds)

6. Poxviridae Family :

The family is divided into several genera. All poxviruses

tend to produce skin lesions. Some are pathogenic for humans (smallpox, vaccinia, molluscum contagiosum); others that are pathogenic for animals can infect humans (cowpox, monkeypox).

RNA Viruses

There are certain generalities about RNA viruses, most of which are the opposite of DNA viruses.

Most RNA viruses are single- stranded (half are positive [+1 stranded, half negative [-1), enveloped, show helical capsid symmetry, and replicate in the cytoplasm:

? Toga
? Corona
? Retro
? Picorna
? Calici
? Reo
? Orthomyxo
? Paramyxo
? Rhabdo
? Bunya
? Arena
? Fibo.

Paramyxoviridae Family

Three genera have been recognised:

1. Paramyxovirus which consists of the Newcastle disease virus, mumps virus and parainfluenza viruses of humans, other mammals and birds.

2. Morbillivirus, containing measles, canine distemper, rinderpest and related viruses.

3. Pneumovirus, containing respiratory syncytial virus of humans and related viruses.

Togaviridae Family

Three genera have been described:

1. Alpha virus, consisting of viruses formerly classified as Group A arboviruses.

2. Rubivirus, consisting of the rubella virus and has no arthropod vector.

3. Pestivirus, consisting of the mucosal disease virus, hog cholera virus and related viruses.

8. Coronaviridae Family Only one genus Coronavirus has been recognized. Members include human corona virus causing upper respiratory disease, avian infectious bronchitis virus, calf neonatal diarrhea corona virus, murine hepatitis virus and related viruses. Most human coronaviruses cause mild acute upper respiratory tract illnesses (colds) but a new coronavirus identified in 2003 causes a severe acute respiratory syndrome (SARS). Toroviruses, which cause gastroenteritis, form a distinct genus.

Reoviridae Family

Icosahedral, nonenveloped viruses, medium-sized (6080 nm), with double layered capsids. Genome consists of double stranded RNA in 10-12 pieces. Three genera have been recognised.

1. Reovirus, containing reoviruses from humans, other mammals and birds.

2. Orbivirus, containing several species of arboviruses such as blue tongue virus, African horse sicknessvirus.

3. Coltivirus includes Colorado tick fever virus of humans.

4. Rotavirus including human rotaviruses, calfdiarrhea virus and related agents. Other genera may have to be defined to include plant and insect viruses belonging to this family.

Q 33. General Characteristics / properties of Viruses.

= Viruses are the smallest known infective agents and

are perhaps the simplest form of life known. Viruses do not possess a cellular organization and they do not fall strictly into the category of unicellular microorganisms. Even the simplest of microorganisms are cells enclosed within a cell wall, containing both types of nucleic acid (DNA and RNA), synthesizing their own macromolecular constituents and multiplying by binary fission.

MAIN PROPERTIES OF VIRUSES

1. Viruses do not have a cellular organization.
2. They contain only one type of nucleic acid, either DNA or RNA but never both.
3. They are obligate intracellular parasites.
4. They lack the enzymes necessary for protein and nucleic acid synthesis and are dependent for replication on the synthetic machinery of host cells.
5. They multiply by a complex process and not by binary fission.
6. They are unaffected by antibacterial antibiotics.

Q 34. Explain the various methods of the cultivation of viruses.

= **CULTIVATION OF VIRUSES :**

Because viruses are obligate intracellular parasites, their growth requires susceptible host cells capable of replicating them. They cannot be grown on any inanimate culture medium. Three methods are employed for the cultivation of viruses:

A. Animal inoculation

B. Embryonated eggs

C. Cell culture.

A. Animal Inoculation

Uses of Animal Inoculation

i. Primary isolation of certain viruses

ii. For the study of pathogenesis, immune response and epidemiology of viral diseases

iii. For the study of oncogenesis.

1. Monkeys

Monkeys were used for the isolation of the poliovirus but find only limited application in virology due to their cost and risk to handlers.

2. Mice

The use of white mice, pioneered by Theiler (1903) extended the scope of animal inoculation greatly. Infant (suckling) mice are very susceptible to coxsackie and arboviruses, many of which do not grow in any other system. Mice may be inoculated by several routes—intracerebral, subcutaneous, intraperitoneal or intranasal. The growth of the virus in inoculated animals may be indicated by death, disease or visible lesions. The viruses are identified by testing for neutralization of their pathogenicity for animals, by standard antiviral sera.

B. EmbrYonated Eggs

The embryonated hen's egg was first used for the cultivation of viruses by Goodpasture (1931) and the method was further developed by Burnet. The embryonated egg (8-11 day old) are inoculated by several routes for the cultivation of viruses such as chorioallantoic membrane (CAM), allantoic cavity, amniotic cavity and yolk sac. After being inoculated, eggs are incubated for 2-9 days.

C. Tissue Culture :

Three types of tissue cultures are available

1. Organ Culture

Small bits of organs can be maintained in vitro for days and weeks, preserving their original architecture and function. Organ cultures are useful for the isolation of some viruses which appear to be highly specialized parasites of certain organs. For example, the tracheal ring organ culture is employed for the isolation of coronavirus, a respiratory pathogen.

2. Explant Culture

Fragments of minced tissue can be grown as 'explant' embedded in plasma clots and was originally known as 'tissue culture'. This method is now seldom employed in virology. Adenoid tissue explant cultures were used for the isolation of adenoviruses.

3. Cell Cultures

This is the type of culture routinely employed for growing viruses. Tissues are dissociated into the component cells by the action of proteolytic enzymes such as trypsin and mechanical shaking. The cells are washed, counted and suspended in a growth medium. Such media will enable most cell types to multiply with a division time of 24-48 hours.

Q 35. Classification of viruses.

= CLASSIFICATION OF VIRUSES

Viruses began to be classified into groups based on their physicochemical and structural features from the early 1950s. Nomenclature and classification are now the official responsibility of the International Committee on Taxonomy of Viruses.

Main Criteria Used for the Classification of Viruses :

1. Type of nucleic acid: Viruses are classified into two main divisions depending on the type of nucleic acid they possess: riboviruses are those containing RNA and deoxyriboviruses are those containing DNA.

2. Number of strands of nucleic acid: Single- or double-stranded, linear, circular, circular with breaks, segmented.

3. Polarity of the viral genome: RNA viruses in which the viral genome can be used directly as messenger RNA are by convention termed 'positive-stranded' and those for which a transcript has first to be made are termed 'negative-stranded.

4. The symmetry of the nucleocapsid.

5. The presence or absence of a lipid envelope.

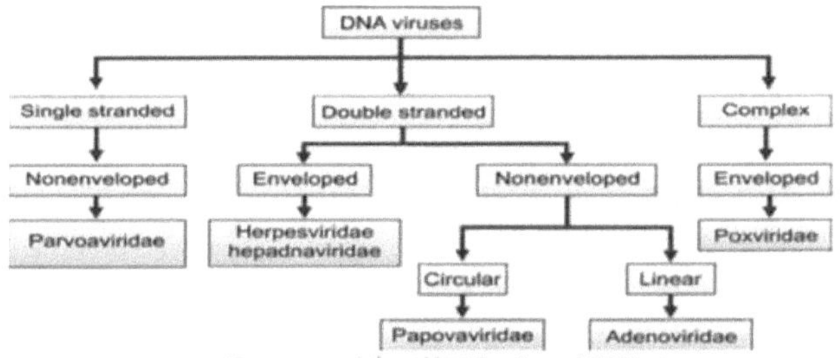

Summary of the classification of DNA viruses

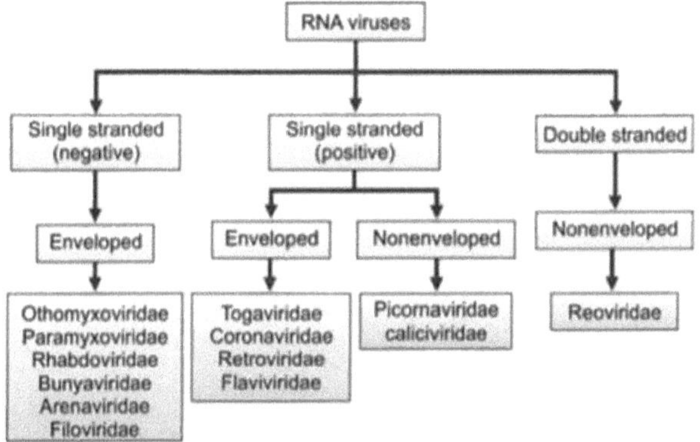

Summary of the classification of RNA viruses

CHAPTER FIVE

IMMUNITY

Q 1.Difference between active & passive immunity.

=

	Active immunity		Passive immunity
1	Produced actively by the immune system of host	1	Received passively by the host and the host's immune system does not participate.
2	Induced by infection or by contacts with immunogen, e.g. vaccines.	2	Conferred by introduction of ready-made antibodies.
3	Immunity develops only after a lag period	3	Immune response-short lived and less effective.
4	Immune response-durable and effective	4	Immunity effective immediately.
5	Immunological memory present. Subsequent challenge with booster dose more effective.	5	No immunological memory. Subsequent administration of antibody less effective due to "immune elimination"
6	Serves no purpose in immunodeficient host	6	Applicable in immunodeficient host
7	Used for prophylaxis to increase body resistance	7	Used for treatment of acute infection.

Table 12.1: Comparison of active and passive immunity

Active immunity	*Passive immunity*
1. Produced actively by host's immune system	1. Received passively. No active host participation
2. Induced by infection or by immunogens	2. Readymade antibody transferred
3. Durable effective protection	3. Transient, less effective
4. Immunity effective only after lag period, i.e. time required for generation of antibodies and immunocompetent cells.	4. Immediate immunity
5. Immunological memory present	5. No memory
6. Booster effect on subsequent dose	6. Subsequent dose less effective
7. 'Negative phase' may occur	7. No negative phase
8. Not applicable in the immunodeficient	8. Applicable in immunodeficient

Q 2. Write a short note on Immunoglobulin (Ig)

= **DEFINITION**

Immunoglobulin (Ig)

Immunoglobulins are glycoprotein molecules that are produced by plasma cells in response to an immunogen and which function as antibodies. The immunoglobulins derive their name from the finding that they migrate with globular proteins when antibody-containing serum is placed in an electrical field.

Immunoglobulin classes

The immunoglobulins can be divided into five different classes, based on differences in the amino acid sequences in the constant region of the heavy chains. All immunoglobulins within a given class will have very similar heavy chain constant regions. These differences can be detected by sequence studies or more commonly by serological means (i.e. by the use of antibodies directed to these differences).

IgG - Gamma heavy chains

IgM - Mu heavy chains

IgA - Alpha heavy chains

IgD - Delta heavy chains

IgE - Epsilon heavy chains.

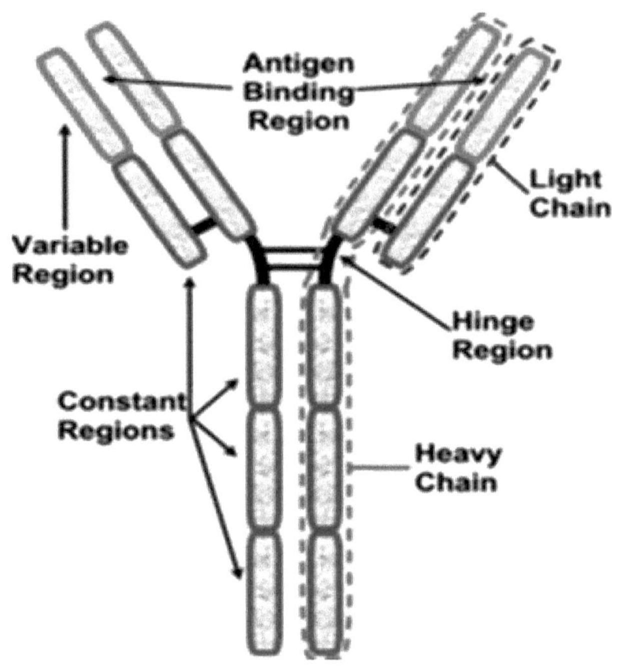

Q 3. WIDAL Test .

= INTRODUCTION OF WIDAL TEST

In 1896 and named after its inventor, Georges-Fernand Widal, is an indirect agglutination test for enteric fever or undulant fever whereby bacteria causing typhoid fever is mixed with a serum containing specific antibodies obtained from an infected individual.

In cases of Salmonella infection, it is a demonstration of the presence of O-soma false-positive result.

Test results need to be interpreted carefully to account for any history of enteric fever, typhoid vaccination, and the general level of antibodies in the populations in endemic areas of the world.

Widal test is a serological test that is done for the diagnosis of typhoid fever caused by Salmonella organism.

This test detects the "O" and "H" antigen of Salmonella typhi and paratyphi A,B and C.

When facilities for culturing are not available, the Widal test is the reliable and can be of value in the diagnosis of typhoid fevers in endemic areas.

CLINICAL SIGNIFICANCE •

Typhoid fever or enteric fever occurs when S. Typhi, S. Paratyphi A, S. Paratyphi B, S. Paratyphi C infect the human body.

• Body responds to this antigenic stuimulus by producing antibodies whose titre rise slowly in early stages, to a maximum and then slowly falls till it is undetectable.

• Persons with typhoid fever carry the bacteria in their bloodstream and intestinal tract.

• Transmitted through the ingestion of food or drink contaminated by the feces or urine of infected people

Q 4. ELISA Test.

= Enzyme-linked Immunosorbent Assay (ELISA)

Enzyme-linked immunosorbent assay, commonly known as ELISA or EIA), is similar in principle to RIA but the radioactive tag used in RIA techniques can be replaced with an enzyme. When this enzyme is linked to an antibody and used to detect and measure other antibodies or antigens, the assay is called the enzyme-linked immunosorbent assay (ELISA). An enzyme conjugated with antibody reacts with a colorless substrate to generate a colored reaction product. Such a substrate is called a chromogenic substrate.

Enzyme-linked immune sorbent assay is highly sensitive, highly specific and less expensive technique used in serology to detect antigens or antibodies.

Types of ELISA

1. Indirect ELISA
2. Sandwich ELISA

(a) Single antibody or direct sandwich ELISA
(b) Double-antibody or indirect sandwich ELISA
3. Competitive ELISA

USES OF ELISA

ELISA is a simple and versatile technique. It needs only microliter quantities of reactants. ELISA has been used to detect antigens and antibodies of various microorganisms.

Examples

Parasites

- Entamoeba histolytica antigens in feces
- Toxoplasma antigens in the patient serum.

Bacteria

- Haemophilus influenzae antigens in spinal fluid
- β-haemolytic streptococcal antigen in spinal fluid
- Labile enterotoxin of E. coli in stools.

To detect antibody specific for:

- **Mycoplasmas**
- Chlamydiae
- Borrelia burgdorferi.

Viruses

To detect antibody specific for:

- Hepatitis virus antigens
- Herpes simplex viruses 1 and 2
- Respiratory syncytial virus (RSV)
- Cytomegalovirus
- Human immunodeficiency virus (HIV)
- Rubella virus (both IgG and IgM)
- Adenovirus antigens—in nasopharyngeal specimens.

Q 5. Difference between Immediate & Delayed Hypersensitivity .

=

Table 20.1: Distinguishing features of immediate and delayed types of hypersensitivity

Characteristic	Immediate hypersensitivity	Delayed hypersensitivity
1. Time of reaction after challenge with antigen	1. Reaction appears and recedes rapidly.	1. Appears slowly, lasts longer.
2. Induction	2. Induced by antigens or haptens.	2. Antigen or hapten intradermally or with by any route.
3. Immune response	3. Circulating antibodies present and responsible for reaction; 'antibody mediated' reaction.	3. Circulating antibodies may be absent and are not responsible for reaction; 'cell-mediated' reaction.
4. Transfer of hypersensitivity	4. Passive transfer possible with serum.	4. Cannot be transferred with serum; but possible with T cells or transfer factor.
5. Desensitization	5. Desensitization easy, but short-lived.	5. Difficult, but long-lasting.

Q 6. Classify immunoglobulin and write in short about IgG.

= **IMMUNOGLOBULIN CLASSES**

Human serum contain five classes of immunoglobulins—IgG, IgA, IgM, IgD and IgE in the descending order of the concentration.

.

1. Immunoglobulin G (IgG)

1. This is the major immunoglobulin in human serum, accounting for about 80 percent of the total immunoglobulin pool.

2. It has a sedimentation coefficint of 7S and a molecular weight of 150,000.

3. It contains less carbohydrate than other immunoglobulins.

4. The normal serum concentration of IgG is about 8 to 16 mg per ml.

5. It has a half-life of 23 days—the longest of all of the immunoglobulin isotypes.

6. IgG is the predominant immunoglobulin in blood, lymph, peritoneal fluid, and cerebrospinal fluid, and it is distributed nearly equally between extraand intravascular spaces. Therefore, IgG is

particularly suitable for passive immunization done by the transfer of serum containing antibodies (antiserum).

7. Four subclasses of IgG (Ig1, Ig2, Ig3, Ig4) have been recognized. Each subclass possesses a distinct type of γ chain which can be identified with specific antiserum. They constitute about 65 percent, 23 percent, 8 percent and 4 percent respectively of the total human IgG.

8. Catabolism of IgG is unique in that it varies with its serum concentration. When its level is raised, as in chronic malaria, kala-azar or myeloma, the IgG synthesized against a particular antigen will be catabolized rapidly and may result in the particular antibody deficiency. Conversely, in hypogammaglobulilnemia, the IgG given for treatment will be catabolized only slowly.

Functions of IgG

IgG is a very versatile molecule. It may be considered a general purpose antibody, protective against those infectious agents which are active in the blood and tissues.

It is protective against those micro organisms which are active in blood or tissue.

Q7. Types of Vaccines.

= A vaccine [Latin vacca, cow] is a preparation from an

infectious agent that is administered to humans and other animals to induce protective immunity against a

given disease.

Types of Vaccines

1. Live Vaccines

Live vaccines (e.g., BCG, measles, oral polio) are prepared from live (generally attenuated) organisms. These organisms have been passed repeatedly in the laboratory in tissue culture or chick embryos and have lost their capacity to induce full blown disease but retain their immunogenicity. In general, live vaccines are more potent immunizing agents than killed vaccines.

2. Killed (Inactivated) Vaccines

Organisms killed by heat or chemicals, when infected into the body stimulate active immunity. They are usually safe but generally less efficacious than live vaccines.

3. Toxoids

Certain organisms produce exotoxins, e.g., diphtheria and tetanus bacilli. The toxins produced by these organisms are detoxicated and used in the preparation of vaccines.

4. Cellular Fractions

Vaccines, in certain instances, are prepared from extracted cellular fractions, e.g., meningococcal vaccine from the polysaccharide antigen of the cell wall, the pneumococcal vaccine from the polysaccharide contained in the capsule of the organism and hepatitis B polypeptide vaccines. Although the duration of experience with these vaccines is limited, their efficacy and safety appear to be high.

5. Mixed or Combined Vaccine

If more than one kind of immunizing agent is included in the vaccine, it is called a mixed or combined vaccine. The following are some of the well-known combinations:

DPT (Diphtheria-pertussis-tetanus)

DT (Diphtheria-tetanus)

DP (Diphtheria-pertussis)

DPT and typhoid vaccine

MMR (Measles, mumps and rubella)

DPTP (DPT plus inactivated polio).

7. DNA Vaccines

A DNA vaccine elicits protective immunity against a microbial pathogen by activating both branches of the immune system: humoral and cellular. Long-lasting memory are cells also are generated.

Examples: At present, there are human trials under way with several different DNA vaccines against malaria, AIDS, influenza, hepatitis B, and herpesvirus.

Q 8.Explain National immunization scheduled.

= National Immunization Schedule

The National Immunization Schedule is given in Table :

The first visit may be made when the infant is 6 weeks old; the second and third visits, at intervals of 1 to 2 months. Oral polio vaccine may be given concurrently with DPT. BCG can be given with any of the three doses but the site for the injection should be different.

The schedule also covers immunization of women during pregnancy against tetanus.

Table 82.1: National immunization schedule

a.	For infants		
	At birth (for institutional deliveries	-	BCG and OPV-O dose
	At 6 weeks	-	BCG (if not given at birth)
		-	DPT-1 and OPV-1
	At 10 weeks	-	DPT-2 and OPV-2
	At 14 weeks	-	DPT-3 and OPV-3
	At 9 months	-	Measles
b.	At 16—24 months	-	DPT and OPV
c.	At 5—6 years	-	DT-the second dose of DT should be given at an interval of one month if there is no clear history or documented evidence of previous immounization with DPT
d.	At 10 and 16 years	-	Tetanus Toxoid - The second dose of TT vaccine should be given at an interval of one month if there is no clear history or documented evidence of provious immunization with DPT, DT or TT vaccines
e.	For pregnant women		
	Early in pregnancy	-	TT-1 or Booster
	One month after TT-1—TT-2		

Note: i. Intreval between 2 dose should not be less than one month.
ii. Minor cough, colds and mild fever are not a contraindication to vaccination.
iii. In some states, Hepatitis B vaccine is given as routine immunization.

National immunization scheduled.

Q 9. Agglutination.

= Agglutination.

It is an antigen-antibody reaction, in which a particulate antigen combines with its antibody in the presence of electrolytes at an optimal temperature and pH, resulting in visible clumping of particles. It differs from precipitation in which soluble antigen is present in contrast to particulate antigen of agglutination. Principles governing agglutination are the same as that of precipitation. Agglutination occurs when antigen and antibody are present in optimal proportions. Lattice formation hypothesis holds good for agglutination too. The zone phenomenon may occur when either an antigen or an antibody is in excess.

Types of Agglutination Reaction

1. Slide Agglutination

Test A uniform suspension of antigen is made in a drop of saline on a slide or tile and a drop of the appropriate antiserum is added. Clumping occurs instantly or within seconds when agglutination test is positive.

Uses:

(i) It is a routine procedure to identify the bacterial trains isolated from clinical specimens. One example is to jdentify Salmonella species.

(ii) Itisalsoused for blood groupingand crossmatching.

2. Tube Agglutination Test

This is a standard quantitative method for determination of antibodies. Serum is diluted serially by doubling dilution in test tubes. An equal volume of a particulate antigen is added to all tubes. The highest dilution of scrum at which agglutination occurs is antibody titre. Tube agglutination is routinely employed for antibody detection in diagnosis of Lyphoid (Widal test). brucellosis and typhus fevers (Weil-Felix reaction).

Q 10.Immunoprophylaxix .

= Medical definition of immunoprophylaxis: the prevention of disease by the production of active or passive immunity.

Immunoprophylaxix Protection against infectious diseases by (immunization) acquired by the individual either passively or actively:

I. **Passive acquired immunity**
II. **II- Active acquired immunity**

I- Passive acquired immunity

Ready made Ab transferred to individual giving rapid protection and short lasting immunity:

a-Naturally acquired passive immunity Occurs when antibody are transferred from mother to fetus (IgG) or in colostrum (Ig A).

b- Artificially acquired passive immunity Short-term immunization by injection of antibodies,

For examples: - injection of antitoxic serum for treatment of diphtheria or tetanus. - injection of gamma globulin that are not produced by recipient's cells, to hypogammaglobulin children .

II- Active acquired immunity

Individual actively produces his own Ab. Immunity develop slowly and long lasting due to development of immunological memory:

a-Natural active acquired immunity The person becomes immune as a result of previous exposure to a live pathogen

b-Artificially active acquired immunity A vaccine stimulates a primary response against the antigen without causing symptoms of the disease.

Q 12. Difference between oral (OPV) & killed (IPV) Polio vaccine .

=

Property	OPV	IPV
Mode of administration	By mouth	Injectable
Type	Live attenuated	Inactivated
Gastrointestinal tract immunity	Yes	No
Virus shed in feces	Yes	No
Requirements for transport and storage	Strict	Not strict
Ability to revert	Yes	No

Difference between oral (OPV) & killed (IPV) Polio vaccine .

Q 13. Difference between IgG & IgM .

=

IgG	IgM
IgG refers to a class of immunoglobulins containing the most abundant type of antibodies that circulate in the blood	IgM refers to a class of immunoglobulins composed of a pentamer structure that includes the primary antibodies released early in the immune response
Refers to the immunoglobulin G	Refers to the immunoglobulin M
Produced at the latest stages of the immune response	Produced in the early stages of the immune response
Four subclasses of IgG are IgG1, IgG2, IgG3, and IgG4	Lack subclasses
Smaller than IgM (150 kDa)	Larger in size (970 kDa)
Monomer	Pentamer
Consists of two antigen binding sites	Consists of ten antigen binding sites
Most abundant type of immunoglobulin	Less abundant than IgG

Difference between IgG & IgM

Q 13. Define immunity.

= **DEFINITION**

Immunity Latin immunis, free of burden] refers to the resistance exhibited by the host towards injury caused by microorganisms and their products.

Or

Immunity is the capacity of multicellular organisms to resist harmful microorganisms.

Q 14. Classify the immunity types .

= **CLASSIFICATION**

Immunity against infectious diseases is of different types. The discrimination between self and nonself, and the subsequent destruction and removal of foreign material, is accomplished by two arms of immune system, the innate (or "natural") immune system, and the adaptive (or "acquired"), specific immune system.

Immunity

i. Innate (or natural) immunity

a. Nonspecific

Species

Racial

Individual

b. Specific

Species

Racial

Individual

ii. Acquired (or adaptive) immunity

a. Active

Natural

Artificial

b. Passive

Natural

Artificial

Q 15. Explain the mechanism of innate immunity.

= **Mechanisms of Innate Immunity**

1. Epithelial Surfaces

i) Skin

It not only acts as a mechanical barrier to microorganisms but also provides bactericidal secretions. The high concentration of salt in drying sweat, the sebaceous secretions and long chain fatty acids contribute to bactericidal activity.

(ii) Respiratory tract

The inhaled particles are arrested in the nasal passages on the moist mucous membrane surfaces. The mucous secretions of respiratory tract act as trapping mechanism and hair like cilia propels the particles towards the pharynx where it is swallowed or coughed out. The cough reflex acts as an important defence mechanism,

iii) Intestinal tract

The mouth possesses saliva which has an inhibitory effect on many micro-organisms. Some bacteria may be swallowed and are destroyed by acidic pH of gastric juices.

(iv) Conjunctiva

Tears have a major role by flushing away bacteria and other dust particles. In addition, lysozyme present in tears has a bactericidal action.

v) The Genitourinary tract

The flushing action of urine eliminates bacteria from the urethra . The acidic pH of vaginal secretions in female, due to the fermentation of glycogen by lactobacillus (normal flora), renders vagina free of many pathogens.

2. Antibacterial Substances

Besides specific antibody formation, there are number of nonspecific antibacterial substances present in blood and tissues. These substances are properdin, complement, lysozyme etc.

3. Cellular Factors

Once the infective agent has crossed the barrier of epithelial surfaces, the tissue factors come into play for defence.)

Q 16.Write a short note on IgM.

= Immunoglobulin M (IgM)

1. About 10 percent of normal serum Igs consists of this class.

2. It is a heavy molecule (19S; MW 900,000 to 1,000,000 daltons, hence called 'millionaire molecule').

3. The normal serum level of IgM is 1.2 mg/ml.

4. It has a half-life of about 5 days.

5. IgM is the first immunoglobulin to appear after
exposure to an antigen.

6. In the circulation, IgM exists as a pentamer of five four-chain units. The five identical IgM monomers are connected to each other by a polypeptide joining J chain. Polymerization of the subunits depends upon the presence of the J chain as with IgA. Monomeric IgM and IgD are present on the surface of mature, naive B cells.

7. IgM contains 10 Fab fragments, and thus 10 antigenbinding sites. Though the theoretical valency is ten, this is observed only with small haptens. The effective valency falls to five with larger antigens, probably due to steric hindrance.

Most of IgM (80 percent) is intravascular in distribution.

8. Phylogenetically IgM is the oldest Ig class. IgM is the
first class of antibody produced during the primary immune response. It is also the earliest to be synthesized by fetus beginning by about 20 weeks of age.

As it cannot cross the placental barrier, the presence of IgM in the fetus or newborn indicates intrauterine infection. Its detection is, therefore, useful for the diagnosis of congenital infections such as syphilis, rubella, human immunodeficiency virus (HIV) infection and toxoplasmosis.

9. They are relatively short-lived hence their demonstration in the serum indicates recent infection.

10. Treatment of serum with 0.12 M 2-mercaptoethanol selectively destroys IgM without affecting IgG antibodies.This provides a simple method for differential estimation of IgG and IgM

antibodies.

11. Isohemagglutinins (anti-A and anti-B) and antibodies to S. Typhi O antigen and Wassermann reaction antibodies in syphilis are usually IgM.

12. IgM agglutinates bacteria, activates complement by the classical pathway, and enhances the ingestion of pathogens by phagocytic cells. IgM is normally restricted to the intravascular space because of its high molecular weight.

Contact Details

For more Than 10 copies contact on following no : (Discount Granted 25 - 35 %)

Mobile no : 9130024431.

Email : rutwik61@gmail.com

Thanks You .

Best of luck ...

Book Available On

Book available on

Printed by Libri Plureos GmbH in Hamburg, Germany